D0198728

I Never Gave My
Consent

ISLINGTON LIBRARIES

3 0120 02691243 6

I Never Gave My Consent

Consent

A Schoolgirl's Life
Inside the Telford Sex Ring

Holly Archer

With Geraldine McKelvie

**SIMON &
SCHUSTER**

London · New York · Sydney · Toronto · New Delhi

A CBS COMPANY

First published in Great Britain by Simon & Schuster UK Ltd, 2016
A CBS COMPANY

Copyright © 2016 by Holly Archer

This book is copyright under the Berne Convention.
No reproduction without permission.
All rights reserved.

The right of Holly Archer to be identified as the author of this
work has been asserted in accordance with sections 77 and
78 of the Copyright, Designs and Patents Act, 1988.

3 5 7 9 10 8 6 4 2

Simon & Schuster UK Ltd
1st Floor
222 Gray's Inn Road
London WC1X 8HB

www.simonandschuster.co.uk

Simon & Schuster Australia, Sydney
Simon & Schuster India, New Delhi

The author and publishers have made all reasonable efforts to contact
copyright-holders for permission, and apologise for any omissions or errors in
the form of credits given. Corrections may be made to future printings.

While this book gives a faithful account of the author's experiences,
names and some details have been changed to protect the identity and
privacy of certain individuals. Holly Archer is a pseudonym.

A CIP catalogue record for this book
is available from the British Library

Paperback ISBN: 978-1-4711-5702-8
Ebook ISBN: 978-1-4711-5703-5

Typeset in the UK by M Rules
Printed and bound by CPI Group (UK) Ltd, Croydon, CR0 4YY

Simon & Schuster UK Ltd are committed to sourcing paper that is
made from wood grown in sustainable forests and support the Forest Stewardship
Council, the leading international forest certification organisation. Our books
displaying the FSC logo are printed on FSC certified paper.

Contents

Prologue

As the room slowly slid into focus, all I could make out was a sea of faces around me. They were grinning, laughing, mocking me, but I couldn't hear what they were saying. I felt like I was drowning, gasping for air as my lungs filled with water.

They'd only bought me one drink but somehow I'd blacked out on the way here, zoning in and out of consciousness as they carried my limp body from the car and dumped me on the filthy mattress.

Now I was naked.

I couldn't quite lift my head to check where they'd left my clothes and I could feel the panic rising in my throat. My limbs were like jelly but, if I concentrated really hard, I could move my leg just a little to kick out in protest. As I did, I felt a hand collide with my face. One of the men grabbed me by the shoulders.

'The more you kick off,' he said, 'the longer it'll take.'

So I had no choice.

I had no choice, as a group of strange men, some old enough to be my dad, pinned my arms and legs to the horrible, rotten, bare mattress they'd laid me on against my will. One by one they climbed on top of me and did the unthinkable, as the sights of the filthy damp room swam before my eyes and tears streamed down my face.

I'm not sure how many of them there were. There could have been eight, possibly nine. All I know is that by the time the last of them was on top of me, groping at my chest with his wrinkly hands, the smell of stale cigarettes on his breath, the feeling in my legs was beginning to return and the searing pain down below had started to take hold.

When they'd finally finished, I was able to stumble from the mattress and into the bathroom, where I wrapped myself in a tiny towel. Without a second thought for my modesty or the blood that gushed down my legs, I made for the door and fell, screaming, into the night.

I was barely sixteen the night I was brutally gang-raped.

It sounds shocking, of course, but it wasn't the first time I'd been seized by strange men and violated in the most horrific way imaginable. Far from it. For me, sexual abuse was a daily reality. My teenage years were punctuated by rape and beatings, as I was passed around paedophiles like a piece of meat.

Why did I do it? you might ask. Why didn't I say no? Why didn't I just go home? If only it was that easy. They owned me. If I tried to hide, they'd find me. If I tried to resist, they'd hound me with phone calls, beat me until I was black and blue and threaten to tell my mum I was a prostitute.

And if that didn't work?

'If you don't do what we tell you,' they'd say, voices always hushed, 'we'll come for your sisters.'

I was trapped but, for a long time, I thought it was my fault. I believed them when they called me a slut and told me how worthless I was. I even believed I was a prostitute because they'd sometimes chuck me a few quid after they'd raped me.

Now, of course, I know there's no way I could have been a prostitute because *I was a child* – an abused child. Even if I'd wanted to sleep with all of these disgusting men, I wasn't capable of making that choice because I was too young.

None of this was my fault, but it's taken me a long time to realise that. It's been a painful journey, but I've finally come to accept I wasn't to blame.

This is my story. My story of how I never gave my consent.

I

Carefree Days

My childhood was about as normal and carefree as you could imagine.

I was born in the sprawling market town of Telford on an unremarkable spring day in the late eighties. My home lay in Shropshire, near the Welsh border, off the newly built M54 motorway, about thirty miles from Birmingham. I was the third child for my mum, Karen, and my dad, Joe, coming along a few years after Gemma, my older sister, and Liam, my older brother.

A few days later, Mum and Dad were allowed to take me home to their three-bedroomed, semi-detached house. There wasn't much to the district itself. The high street had a few shops and pubs, but the surrounding area was really pretty: lots of woodland and countryside – trees and fields and rolling hills. I suppose part of the attraction was that nothing really happened there, or so everyone thought. A nice place to raise children, you might think.

Like many places in the Midlands, Telford had become home to a scattering of immigrants throughout the latter part of the twentieth century. Asians, mostly, from Pakistan and China, but also some from Bangladesh. New convenience shops and exotic restaurants and takeaways gradually started to pop up in parts of the town.

Some of the Asian families were really strict. Many didn't let their children drink or stay out late and most had to have an arranged marriage to someone chosen by their parents. That's not to say some didn't bend the rules, sneaking off to the pub or getting with a secret English girlfriend.

Of course, there were a few small-minded people who ranted about how they were coming from all sorts of places to steal everyone's jobs, but to be honest I think they were few and far between. Mum and Dad, and most people they knew, were happy to live and let live. They were much more preoccupied with our little family and making ends meet with three demanding children under the age of five.

I guess I was lucky that I was too young to realise my parents' relationship was already starting to sour by the time I came along. I'm not sure quite what went wrong – perhaps they'd met when they were too young and the pressure of raising three young children was all too much. But when I was just two, they decided to divorce.

I suppose my earliest memories are among the few negative thoughts I have when I remember my childhood, but they're hazy, just snapshots of Mum and Dad arguing and Mum taking us kids to stay at Nan and Granddad's for a few weeks. By the time we returned, Dad was gone. He spent a few weeks sleeping on friends' sofas, before getting a little flat. I can't really remember much, but my siblings said he seemed a little down for a while, before he picked himself up and dusted himself off.

Life went on. We stayed with Mum during the week and visited Dad at the weekends, though he was only down the road, so we could see him whenever we liked.

Things were quite simple back in the early nineties. No one had an iPad or an Xbox, but it didn't seem to matter. As a toddler, I loved sitting in Mum's back garden, watching ladybirds scuttle across the slabs. I was mesmerised by them and I'd often pick them up and stare at them before they wriggled out of my hands. One day, though, curiosity got the better of me and I decided to drop one in a huge puddle that had gathered close to Mum's back door. Of course it drowned and I felt awful. The poor ladybird!

As we got older, Gemma became motherly towards Liam and me. She'd always try to make the rules and tell us what to do, especially at the weekend when we were at Dad's. Liam and I didn't like this one bit, and we ganged up on her. We had a little pack of marbles and we'd hit them really hard against the wall, so they would rebound and hit her legs. She'd cry, and we'd laugh our heads off. Normal sibling stuff, of course, but now I feel terrible, as Gemma and I are so close.

It was around this time I started school. Although I was boisterous and lively around my siblings, at school I was quite shy. At first I found the whole experience a little overwhelming. I struggled to keep up with my classmates because I couldn't see the blackboard properly and, while my peers managed to grasp the letters of the alphabet with ease, I kept mixing mine up. I was scared to ask for help in case the teacher shouted at me, so I struggled in silence.

By this time, Mum had met a new man named Phil. I don't

really remember the first time he came round, or how he was introduced to us. I just remember him being there. Unlike a lot of kids in our position, we didn't view him as a threat or an outsider. We took to him immediately, mainly because he was a bit of a joker. His favourite trick was to attach a Barbie or an Action Man doll to a washing line, which he'd hang from my bedroom window, and we'd watch as it slid to the ground.

'It's the death slide!' I'd giggle. 'Do it again, Phil!'

When we were at Mum's, we lived for the outdoors. We'd go into the woods for long walks, giggling as we skipped over branches and stones and listening to the chatter of the birds overhead. When autumn came, we'd gather conkers and nuts, all competing to see who could collect the most.

One of the places we loved to walk was the Wrekin, a big hill about five miles west of Telford. As we clambered to the top, our little jackets zipped up to our necks, we thought we'd climbed the highest mountain in the world. The views from the top, granted, are pretty stunning – you can see as many as seventeen counties on a clear day, well into Wales and beyond. Back then, we thought we could just about see the whole world. Now when I think of the Wrekin my memories are far less joyful and innocent – but that would all come much later.

Back then, when I thought of the future, I only thought of nice things. Mum hadn't worked until us kids all went off to school, but by now she had a little shop job and there was a bit more money to go around. Phil worked in a local factory and together they managed to save up enough to take us to Majorca for a week. None of us had ever been on a plane before and we were so excited you'd have thought we were flying to the moon. We could hardly sit still in our seats!

I was captivated by the air hostesses. They were so composed and calm and the smile never left their perfectly made-up faces. Of course, they were just doing their job, but I thought they looked like they were having the time of their lives.

'Imagine if you got to go on a plane every single day,' I whispered to Liam. 'How cool would that be?'

From that moment on, I decided I wanted to be an air hostess as soon as I left school. I'd spend hours dreaming of all the glamorous locations I'd jet off to and all the exciting people I'd meet.

It wasn't long before Mum and Phil decided to get married. I guess I was pleased, because I liked Phil, but I wasn't happy when they announced the date and it was the day before my eighth birthday. They'd met on that day a few years previously and they'd decided it would be nice to have their wedding on the anniversary. Like most children, I wasn't pleased at the idea of my thunder being stolen.

'That's not fair!' I huffed. 'You'll be obsessed with your wedding and you'll forget all about my birthday. I can't believe you're doing this to me.'

Mum rolled her eyes. 'Of course we won't forget about your birthday, Holly,' she replied, as patiently as she could. 'You'll get all of your presents in the morning, as usual. And you and Gemma will get to be bridesmaids. I'm going to make you a beautiful dress. How does that sound?'

I folded my arms, refusing to wipe the frown from my face as I weighed up the deal on the table.

'And,' Mum added, 'Phil and I have agreed you can each bring a friend.'

With that I relaxed slightly as I mulled over who I would invite. Although I was still struggling with my schoolwork, I had come out of my shell a little and made some friends. I couldn't decide if I should invite Joanna, my best friend from my class, or Carly, a girl I'd met playing football in the street with Liam. Carly was often round our way because her gran looked after her. In the end I decided on Joanna. Carly was nice, but Joanna was just a bit cooler. I knew some of the other kids laughed at Carly because she was a bit chubby, and her mum still did her hair in these really embarrassing long, blonde plaits that stretched all the way down to her waist.

Mind you, I was carrying a bit of puppy fat myself – not that I cared much for my appearance. As I was a bit of a tomboy, I thought I looked stupid in my bridesmaid's dress. It was cream with pink roses and a big pink bow and it made me feel all itchy and uncomfortable. Mum was really proud of it but I felt like an idiot and couldn't wait to get back into my tracksuit.

I suppose I started to think more about how I looked around Year Five. I was only nine but my boobs had started to come on. I developed quicker than the other girls in my class, but I hated my new womanly body with a passion. It didn't seem to fit me, as I still felt like a timid little girl. Some of my classmates were desperate to wear a bra and start their periods, and talked about it non-stop, but I just felt embarrassed, so I hid my chest under baggy T-shirts and jumpers as I'd always done, hoping no one would notice any difference.

It was an intense time, as Mum had started to notice I wasn't keeping up with my schoolwork. She couldn't understand why I seemed bright and articulate when I spoke but my written work was poor. I was miles behind Gemma and Liam, who were both top of the class. Eventually she got my eyes tested and I got glasses. It was a big relief, as I could finally see the blackboard when we were doing sums and spelling, but it still didn't solve the problem completely. After a few tests, I was diagnosed with a mild form of dyslexia.

I've always had a determined streak and, once I set my mind to something, I usually refuse to stop until I've made it happen. I decided I was going to catch up with my schoolwork as quickly as I could, and I enlisted Gemma's help as she was great at spelling and seemed so much cleverer than me. She agreed to help me, but she certainly showed me some tough love. Every Saturday, when we went to Dad's, I had to learn to spell a new word.

'Today, your word is junior,' she said, one afternoon, as we sat on the floor, pencil poised in my hand. 'Come on, write it down. J-U-N-I-O-R.'

I did as I was told, carefully forming each letter with my pencil.

'OK, give me that,' she said, snatching my notebook from me and ripping the page from it. 'Now, do it yourself.'

'Spell it myself?' I said. 'But it's really hard, I can't . . .'

'Yes, you can,' Gemma insisted. 'If you can't spell it by dinner, you're not having any.'

My mouth fell open in shock, but I did as I was told. Of course, Dad would never have denied me my dinner because I couldn't spell a certain word, but I wasn't taking any chances. It took me dozens of attempts, but I finally got it.

After that, I sort of got back on track with my schoolwork and my teachers even began to tell Mum that I was clever, which made me feel a little better, especially as it would soon be time to start secondary school. In preparation for this milestone, most of the girls in my class had started to experiment with make-up and nail varnish. Although I looked more grown-up than most of them, with my already noticeable bust, I didn't care a jot about looking glamorous – quite the opposite. I was still hiding my curves underneath baggy tracksuits and I preferred to spend my evenings playing football with Liam and his mates than painting my nails and staring at the mirror. I couldn't imagine anything more boring.

It sounds a bit cheesy, but back then our evenings were like something out of a storybook: big neighbourhood football matches that went on for hours and hours until the sun started to set and we were called in by our parents, exhausted and splattered with mud, but completely content. Joanna and the girls in my class didn't much like playing football, but Carly always came along. All of the kids who played were great mates back then and it seemed inconceivable that any of us could come to any harm in our tight-knit community.

But just before I started secondary, my world was turned on its head – or so it seemed. Mum sat us all down and explained we were going to have a little brother or sister. While Liam and Gemma took the news of her pregnancy in their stride, I was far from impressed. As the baby of the family, I viewed it almost as a slight. Phil had no biological children and he and Mum longed to have a baby together, but I couldn't accept that.

'Am I not enough for you?' I wailed, melodramatically, as I stomped off to my room.

Mum came upstairs to try to talk things through with me, but I was having none of it. She already had three children. In my book, to want a fourth was plain greedy.

When baby Lauren came along a few months later, things did change a little. I had to admit she was really cute, but even as a baby she was quite independent. Unlike most kids, she didn't need attention constantly and, sometimes, she didn't want us older kids to pick her up, and that really grated on me. Now, of course, I see that she was just a baby but it didn't stop me resenting her a little. Frustrated that we weren't Mum's sole focus, I'd spend more and more time outside playing with Liam and Carly and our mates.

'How's your little sister?' Carly would ask.

'Boring,' I'd say with a shrug. 'She doesn't do anything.'

Thankfully, by the time Mum became pregnant with my youngest sister, Amy, I'd matured slightly. By this time, I was twelve. Amy and I bonded as soon as she was born and I'd rush home from school to kiss and cuddle her and play games. As much as I loved Lauren, I felt a real connection with Amy and, from day one, I was super-protective of her. I just couldn't bear the idea that anyone could hurt her, or that she'd come to any harm.

Sometimes Mum would let me wheel Amy's buggy around Telford when we went shopping and I'd just about burst with pride. By the time I was thirteen, I guess I looked a little bit older, because of my boobs and my maturing body. Often people would coo over Amy before stopping in their tracks and hesitantly asking if she was my daughter.

'No!' I'd gasp. 'She's my sister. I don't have a baby. I'm only thirteen!'

I'd giggle as the relief spread over their faces. The idea of being a teenage mum horrified me, as of course to get pregnant you'd have to have sex. I knew the facts of life but I had very little interest in boys, and sex just seemed, well, a bit minging. There was plenty of time for all that, in my opinion. Even the idea of kissing a boy filled me with horror.

Most of my friends thought differently, though. None of them were having sex – far from it – but they'd sit and gossip in class about which boys they thought were fit and who they wanted to snog at the underage discos we went to in the dingy snooker hall in Telford. It was all really awkward. We'd stand at opposite ends of the room until one of the boys was brave enough to shuffle over and ask one of the girls to dance to some awful chart song that was all the rage back then. The one that really sticks in my mind when I think of those times is 'Blue' by Eiffel 65 because it sounds like it's being sung by a squeaky, strangled robot. How we ever thought such music was cool I'll never know.

It was there I had my first kiss, although I was kind of peer-pressured into it.

'That lad, Ryan, fancies you,' my friend Jayne said. 'You should snog him.'

She pointed to a weedy-looking guy our age with mousy brown hair, standing awkwardly at the other side of the room.

As soon as I met his eye, he looked away and stared at his shoes.

I could feel my face blushing scarlet. 'I don't know . . .'

'Come on, Holly,' she said. 'You've never snogged anyone before. Everyone is doing it. Just get it over with.'

I sighed and shrugged my shoulders. I didn't particularly want to snog Ryan, but neither did I want to be left behind and be a laughing stock because I'd never kissed anyone and all of my mates had. Every teenager knows the feeling, I'm sure.

We awkwardly edged towards each other through the room of sweaty, spotty teenagers, and Ryan murmured something that sounded like hello – not that I could hear him over the music. He put his arms around my waist and, before I knew it, he'd stuck his tongue down my throat. I don't think he'd ever kissed anyone before either, because it was really sloppy. We pulled apart after about ten seconds and went back to our separate groups of friends. All I can remember thinking is, thank God that's over. I was in no hurry to kiss anyone else.

Ali

In the autumn of that year, just after I'd snogged Ryan, things started to change. By now Liam was almost sixteen and we'd gradually started to drift apart. While he and his mates had once loved playing football in the street, they'd all grown up a bit, and kicking a ball around a cul-de-sac with Carly and me seemed a bit uncool. They were much more interested in girls in their own year at school, the kind who dressed up and wore make-up and did their hair. Plus, they all had their GCSEs coming up and some of their parents insisted they stay in at night and revise.

Our neighbourhood football matches became few and far between and they'd soon stop completely, leaving Carly and me at a bit of a loose end.

'Is Liam coming out?' Carly asked one evening when she called for me after school.

'He's got tons of homework,' I replied. 'I don't think he wants to play football with us anymore.'

Carly looked crestfallen. She pushed one of her plaits behind her ear, as she kicked the ground beneath her feet. 'What are we going to do, then?' she asked.

I shrugged. Suddenly, my street seemed much more boring than it had before. There were still kids out playing in gardens and on the pavement, but they were much younger than us and came across as a bit babyish. Carly was still really young for her age and I think she'd have joined them if she could, but I felt a little self-conscious. I knew my friends from high school would laugh if they saw me hanging around with people who still went to primary school.

'I dunno,' I said. 'What do you want to do?'

Carly's face lit up. 'Let's walk into town,' she suggested. 'There are some fit lads from my school who are always hanging around there.'

Hearing Carly talk about 'fit lads' stopped me in my tracks. It was the first time I'd ever heard her say anything like that and it sounded funny. Carly still looked like she was ten or eleven, with the plaits that fell to her waist and the rolls of puppy fat that spilled over her tracksuit bottoms. I'd become a little more image-conscious since starting high school. If truth be told, I was still happiest kicking a ball around in a tracksuit, but quite a few girls in my class had started to bleach their hair and I'd decided to follow suit, but I'd only done it because it was the fashion, not because I particularly wanted any of the boys at school to notice.

'If you want,' I answered, with a shrug. I wasn't really bothered about meeting any lads. I wasn't in any rush to have another sloppy kiss with an awkward boy who could barely look me in the eye. But I was a bit bored, and it was something to do.

It didn't take us long to walk into the centre, as it's such a small place. We walked as far as the local church, an old grey building with a big graveyard next to it. My family wasn't religious, so I'd never been inside, but there was a little bench just a few yards away.

'Will we sit here for a bit?' Carly asked.

I agreed, but we ended up sitting there for about an hour and a half, chatting about silly teenage things, like who had fallen out with whom, until it was time to go home. This became a bit of a nightly routine after that. Carly would call for me after we'd had dinner and done our homework and we'd walk to the bench outside the church. It was all very innocent.

I never saw any of the lads from Carly's school, though, and I began to wonder if they really hung around the church, or if they were just having her on. Carly was gullible like that. As much as I liked her, I was glad she didn't go to my school because I was pretty sure she'd get picked on and I knew I'd be a target too, if I was her mate.

So, in the end, I suppose it all kind of happened by accident.

We were walking through the town as normal when we caught sight of two distant figures, sitting at our usual spot on the bench.

'Carly!' one of them shouted, before we could get a good look at them. 'Carly! Oi!'

Carly pretended not to hear him and I could see her cheeks starting to burn.

'Do you know them?' I asked.

'Just keep walking,' she said.

But as we got closer to the bench, two faces came into view. The first boy looked way older than us. He was really tall, I'd guess around six feet, and had a smattering of stubble – more a five o'clock shadow than a real beard. His hair was gelled to perfection, with a little flick at the front, as was the fashion back then. I could tell his clothes were really expensive: cream jeans and a cream corduroy jacket, with sheepskin round the edges. I suppose he was an all right-looking lad, but I definitely didn't fancy him, although he made me feel suddenly self-conscious in my loose-fitting jeans and top. The second boy looked closer to our age but was really short and fat, with a round, podgy face and tiny black eyes. It didn't really register with me on a conscious level that they both looked Asian, probably of Pakistani origin.

We shuffled past the two boys uneasily, unsure which direction to head in, as they were sitting on our bench. I could feel both pairs of eyes scanning my body, smirking as they looked us up and down. It made me feel really weird, but I wasn't sure why. I just didn't like it.

'Hey, Carly!' the taller boy shouted again. 'Who's your friend? Aren't you gonna stop and talk to me?'

I turned to Carly, expecting her to say nothing and walk on, but she'd stopped. I shot her a confused look, but she pretended not to notice.

'Oh, hey, Ali,' she said, casually.

The taller boy smirked and folded his arms. 'Who's your friend?' he asked again.

'This is Holly,' Carly said. 'She doesn't go to our school.'

I was standing around a foot away from Ali, but the scent of his aftershave wandered into my nostrils and I wrinkled my nose. He looked like a fully grown man. Surely he couldn't still be at school with Carly? I suddenly remembered the fit lads from school she'd talked about with such bravado, but I couldn't understand how she would have known Ali. He must be in the sixth form, I thought. Why would he have any reason to talk to Carly? It sounds bad, but I guessed he wouldn't be likely to be chatting her up.

'What school do you go to?' Ali asked. It sounded more like a threat than a question.

I told him, and his lip curled into a sneer.

Ali nodded. 'Shithole is it, yeah?'

I shrugged, unsure of the right answer. 'Suppose so,' I ventured.

'How old do you think I am?' he demanded. 'I bet you can't guess.'

His brown eyes bored into me and I felt uneasy under his gaze. There was something really intimidating about him, but I couldn't put my finger on what it was. Of course, like most teenage girls, I was desperate not to appear uncool, and I didn't want Ali and his friend to laugh at me. His friend was also looking at me now, and I looked to Carly pleadingly.

'How old is he, Carly?' I asked.

She giggled. 'Guess. Bet you can't.'

'Guess,' Ali echoed. 'Go on.'

'Seventeen?' I said. 'Eighteen?'

All three of them, Carly included, burst out laughing. I felt a little panicky, as if there was some big joke I wasn't in on. I felt instantly annoyed at Carly – she was supposed to be my friend. Wasn't she on my side? Why was she laughing at me with these weird boys? But then it struck me: Carly had never been popular with boys. It wasn't a very nice thing to say, but she hadn't. She was overweight, not exactly streetwise, and her mum still did her hair. She was a perfect target, really. She'd boasted about fit lads from her school, yet she'd almost walked past them when they shouted her name because she was scared they'd tease her. Now here she was, getting to share in their joke, to laugh along with them. It was just a shame the butt of the joke was me.

'Eighteen?' Ali snorted. 'No, guess again.'

'Sixteen?' I said. 'How am I supposed to know how old you are?'

Carly was still smirking but, when I caught her eye, she looked away again, fixing her gaze on the ground.

'He's thirteen,' said the fat boy.

'Shut it, Naseer,' Ali hissed.

'No way,' I replied, feeling bolder than before. 'You're not thirteen.'

'He is,' said Naseer. 'We're in Year Eight.'

'Year Eight!' I repeated, my voice more high-pitched than I'd intended it to be. By this point, Carly and I were in Year Nine. Ali looked like a fully grown man – it just didn't seem possible that he could be telling the truth. I was convinced he was winding me up. 'You can't be in Year Eight. We're in Year Nine.'

'I know,' he said. 'Carly is the year above me. Honestly, I'm thirteen.'

'He is,' Carly piped up. 'Honestly, he is.'

I wasn't sure if I should believe her or not, so I said nothing. For the next few minutes we made small talk. Naseer went to school with Carly and Ali, so they all quizzed me on who I was and where I lived and what lads I'd been with. I didn't give much away; I just tried to laugh their questions off because I hadn't really been with any lads apart from Ryan, and that hardly counted. I quickly realised that Ali was really loud and liked to show off, while Naseer was just obnoxious and liked to insult everyone. I guess he was probably just insecure about his size and bringing others down made him feel good. Still, it didn't make it seem OK.

After about ten minutes, Naseer turned to Carly.

'Want to go for a walk?' he barked. I could tell it wasn't really a question, more of an order.

Carly's mouth fell open, as if she didn't know what to say, but she soon clamped it shut again.

'Go on, Carly,' Ali coaxed. 'What are you scared of?'

Ali and Naseer started to laugh at her and I looked at the ground. Now the tables had turned and they were focusing on Carly, I could understand why she'd joined in when they laughed at me. It was just a relief not to be the butt of their joke.

'OK,' Carly said, after a few seconds. 'Fine. Let's go for a walk.'

She didn't look back at me as they disappeared behind the church together. I was now alone with Ali, but all I could think was, thank God Naseer didn't ask me to go with him. I was so naive, I didn't have a clue what he'd want Carly to do, but I was selfishly glad she'd be left to find out and not me.

As soon as they were out of earshot, Ali turned to me and started to laugh.

'I bet Carly doesn't even know what a blow job is,' he snorted. 'Not that I'd want a fucking blow job from her.'

I stayed silent as my mind raced at a hundred miles an hour. I didn't know what a blow job was either, but there was no way I was about to admit that, as Ali would tear me to shreds and tell Naseer and they'd think it was a hoot. I guessed it might be something to do with sex and that made my stomach turn. I felt really bad, but I was still relieved Naseer had asked Carly to go with him and not me. Whatever a blow job was, I felt sure I didn't want to give him one.

'What do you think?' he asked. 'Do you think she'll have a clue?' He started to laugh again.

'I dunno,' I said. 'Maybe she'll know. I don't know.'

Ali shook his head. 'No chance. I bet she actually blows his dick instead of sucking it.'

My insides lurched violently as everything fell into place and I realised what Ali was suggesting. I could actually feel bile rising in my throat at the thought and it was all I could do not to gag. Kissing Ryan had been disgusting enough – the thought of doing that to a boy was so minging I could barely get my head around it. I was so innocent I didn't even know that boys were supposed to enjoy that kind of thing, but I didn't say anything because I was scared my response would be the wrong one.

'You're quiet,' Ali said. 'Not got much to say for yourself?'

I giggled nervously. 'Don't be a dick,' I said, as bravely as I could. We made idle chitchat for about five or ten minutes. I didn't say much. I just agreed with everything he said, as he leaned against the park bench in his expensive jacket and boasted about all the things he and Naseer and their mates got up to.

After what seemed like an eternity, I caught sight of Carly

and Naseer walking back round to the front of the church. They weren't side by side, like they had been when they walked off. Carly was walking a little in front of him, her round face whiter than usual. Naseer was smirking behind her back.

'Sorted?' Ali said, as they reached the bench.

'Sorted,' Naseer grinned.

Carly wasn't smiling. 'Holly, let's go to the shop,' she said. 'I really need a drink.'

I was relieved to have an excuse to go, and we walked off without another word. Carly was unusually quiet. I had an idea of what had happened because of what Ali had said, but deep down I didn't think Carly would have the guts to do it. I doubt she'd even kissed a boy at that stage, and if *I* didn't know what a blow job was, there was no way she did.

'What's up with you?' I asked, as breezily as I could.

'Nothing,' she said. She paused for a second, as if she was deep in thought. Then she turned to me and said: 'But guess what I just did?'

I felt my stomach twist a little. 'I dunno, what?'

'I bet you've never done this before,' she said.

The colour had started to return to her cheeks and I realised what was happening. It had just dawned on her she had one up on me, something to boast about, something to make her think she was cooler and more grown-up than I was.

'I sucked his dick.'

Hearing Carly say the words out loud made me feel a bit sick and I couldn't help but grimace.

'Ew,' I said. 'Why? Did he make you? What a dickhead.'

'No,' Carly said. 'I thought it would be a laugh.'

'A laugh?' I blurted out, incredulous. Carly was smiling now, a little smugly. She was starting to enjoy this.

'Yeah,' she said, as we arrived at a shop on the corner of the road home. 'It was really small, though. Tiny actually.' She started to giggle. 'But I really need a drink. I can still taste it a bit in my mouth. It's making me feel a bit sick.'

'God, Carly, too much information,' I said. 'Get me a bottle of Coke while you're in there.'

'Have you ever done it?' Carly said. 'I bet you haven't.'

'Carly,' I said, counting out some ten pence pieces, my voice wavering a little. 'Just get me a Coke.'

If I thought we'd seen the last of Ali and Naseer, I was wrong. A few evenings later, as we walked towards the church on our nightly route, Carly's phone began to ring. She answered it before I could see whose name had flashed up on the screen.

'Oh, OK,' she said. 'We're just walking up now. See you in two minutes.'

'Who was that?' I asked, as she hung up.

'Naseer,' she replied. 'Let's go and meet them. They're at the church now.'

I felt my heart sink. 'Naseer? How did he get your number?'

'Well, I gave it to him, didn't I?' she said. 'The other night. It'll be a laugh, come on.'

I sighed as we walked around the corner to see a group of boys huddled by the bench – *our* bench, or at least it used to be. There were three of them this time. Ali, Naseer and another boy who made me stop in my tracks. He had soft olive skin, a little lighter than the other two, and piercing dark eyes. He looked a bit daft – he was wearing a cap, which barely concealed his dodgy haircut. Curtains, we called it back then. But when I saw him, I felt my stomach flip over. Not in a bad way, the way it had when Ali and Naseer had taken the piss out of me a few nights before. It felt like butterflies, a kind of nervous excitement. He was looking at me too, and my heart started beating a little faster as we stared at each other for a few seconds.

'Hey,' he said, with a warm smile. 'How's it going?'

'Yeah, fine,' I replied, as casually as I could.

I soon discovered his name was Imran and he was a year older than me. Looking back, I guess it was the first time I'd ever felt attracted to a boy and it made my head spin a little, as I didn't really know what to do or how to react. Imran had caught me off guard and I had to try my hardest not to stare at him even more than I already had done. He was really fit, much fitter than Ali or Ryan or any other boy my age.

Ali must have caught me looking at Imran, because he soon became a little snappy.

'It's shit round here,' he said. 'Let's go for a walk.'

As he and Naseer started off along the street, Carly and I followed obediently. Imran was behind us and I had a sudden urge to turn round to look at him, almost to check if he was still there, but I didn't dare in case he thought I was some sort of weirdo. We'd been walking for about half a second when Ali turned round sharply.

'You two can't walk with us,' he said. 'You have to walk behind us. And not too close.'

'Eh?' Carly said, confused. 'What's that all about?'

'You just can't,' said Naseer. 'We can't be seen with you. OK?'

'OK,' we said, exchanging confused glances.

'Meet us up by the other church,' said Ali. 'The big church in town. Wait a few minutes before you follow us.'

I could suddenly sense Imran behind me. His aftershave smelled nicer than Ali's and I could feel the heat of his breath on my neck.

'I can walk with you two,' he said. 'I don't mind.'

Ali shrugged, and he and Naseer set off while the three of us hung back, keeping our distance a little.

'Why can't we walk with them?' Carly asked, as they disappeared around the corner. For effect, she added: 'Dickheads.'

Imran let out a little laugh. 'Because if their dads or uncles see them walking about with girls like you they'll know they're up to no good, that's why.'

'Girls like us?' Carly said. 'What's wrong with us?'

At that moment in time I wished Carly would shut up. I didn't really care why Ali and Naseer couldn't be seen with us – I was just happy Imran was walking with us instead of them, as he seemed so much nicer.

'You're not Muslim,' Imran laughed. 'And guys like Ali and Naseer are supposed to be good Muslim boys. They're supposed to be respectable. And their families think girls like you are trouble.'

'Oh,' I said. 'Right.'

Imran smiled at me, his dark eyes beaming as he fixed them on me. My stomach flipped again. 'But don't worry. My dad doesn't give a shit what I do.'

The Methodist church was a bit more modern, a red-brick building with lots of trees and bushes around it. Ali and Naseer were leaning against the wall.

'Hey, Holly!' Ali said, as we approached. 'Come with me. I want to speak to you.' He gestured to the bushes behind the building. 'Round there.'

I looked to Imran, naively hoping he might tell Ali to leave me alone, but he didn't say anything, so I followed Ali a few paces behind until we were out of sight of the road. We stood looking at each other for a second, as Ali leaned against a tree. He was looking at me expectantly and suddenly everything fell into place. I felt two little beads of sweat prick the back of my neck as it dawned on me that he wanted me to do what Carly had done to Naseer earlier in the week.

'Well?' he said. 'You going to give me a blow job or what?'

I shook my head. 'No, Ali,' I said. 'I'm not doing it. I don't want to.'

He folded his arms and lowered his dark eyebrows. Although he had the face and the build of a man, for the first time he looked a bit like a spoilt child, angry at not getting his own way. My heart was beating a little faster than usual but I was determined to keep calm. All I could think was, please don't make me do it. Please don't. I felt sick just thinking of it. I couldn't help but think of Imran and how I'd rather be standing round the front of the church with him, not hidden away behind some trees with Ali.

'Oh, why not?' he said. He sounded whiny, which would have made me laugh had he been asking me to do something a bit less disgusting. 'You know Carly did it for Naseer.'

'Yeah,' I replied, trying not to stumble over my words. 'Well, I'm not Carly. I don't want to do it.'

We looked at each other for a few seconds, stuck in a sort of deadlock.

'I actually really like you, Holly,' Ali said. 'I think you're really cool. And you're pretty.'

I could feel the blood rushing to my cheeks. No one had ever told me I was pretty before and, I have to admit, I was kind of flattered, as I'd always been self-conscious about my looks, but I still didn't fancy Ali. Not one bit.

'Oh, please, Holly,' he went on. 'I don't just want a blow job. I want you to be my girlfriend.'

'But I don't want to be your girlfriend,' I protested.

Ali looked confused. I could tell that wasn't what he was expecting me to say. I wondered if he'd asked any other girls to be his girlfriend, and if they'd done this to him first.

'But it's not fair,' he said. 'I've come round here with you and we've been away for about five minutes now. I'll be a total joke if Naseer can get a blow job and I can't.'

'What do you mean?' I asked.

'Well, I can't come round here and spend all this time with you and not get a blow job,' he said. 'They'll totally take the piss out of me. Naseer will love it, because he got one from Carly and I couldn't get one from you.'

Suddenly Ali didn't seem as cool and hard as he had before but was now a bit pathetic. Maybe he was just as worried about fitting in as Carly and I were. But I still didn't want to give him a blow job, so I said nothing.

'You're still not going to?' he said, after a few seconds.

I shook my head. 'Nope. Sorry.'

He sighed. 'Well, can you at least pretend you did it?' he said. 'So they don't take the piss? Please?'

I felt myself wavering a bit. I didn't really want Ali to tell his mates I'd given him a blow job, but pretending I'd done it was a whole lot better than actually doing it and, if I played along, he might stop pestering me. What was the worst that could happen? He didn't know any of my mates, apart from Carly, so no one I knew would really find out. He wasn't exactly going to start telling people I'd never met that I was a slag. Was he?

'Oh, OK then,' I said. 'Just this once. Can we go back round now?'

Ali grabbed hold of my arm. 'No, not yet. Wait a few minutes at least. I want them to think it lasted a bit longer than this.'

I didn't really understand what he meant, but I leaned against a tree and resigned myself to waiting a few more minutes.

After a brief silence, Ali said: 'You really don't want to be my girlfriend?'

I shook my head. 'Sorry,' I said. 'I don't.'

'Hmm,' he said. 'OK, fine. Can we be friends?'

'Friends?' I echoed. 'Well, if you want, I suppose so.'

Ali raised an eyebrow and he broke into a little half-smile. 'Yeah, why don't we be friends?'

'Fine,' I said. 'Let's be friends.'

'Well, if we're going to be friends you might as well give me your phone number,' Ali replied. 'You know, so we can text and maybe meet up if we're both around town. Just as friends. Nothing more. Friends.'

He kept saying the word 'friends' and I was beginning to feel confused about what this so-called friendship would involve, but he already had his mobile phone in his hand, ready to type my number in. Hesitantly, I recited it.

Ali's phone made a little beeping noise as he punched in the digits. 'Thanks. I suppose we can go back now. It's been over ten minutes.'

I pushed my way back through the overgrown grass to the car park where Carly was still standing with Naseer and Imran.

'Sorted?' Naseer said, with a smirk. His podgy face had gone red in the cold evening air.

Ali nodded. He was still clutching his phone and wearing a self-satisfied grin. Almost in a whisper, he said, 'Sorted.'

3

How Do They Know Who I Am?

Carly couldn't wait until we were out of earshot of the boys to quiz me about Ali. She grabbed my arm as we walked down the road back towards the first church, and practically squealed in my ear.

'Did you give him a blow job?' she asked, her voice all high-pitched and squeaky, the way it went when she was excited. She sounded so childish – more like a little girl asking me what doll I'd got for my birthday than whether or not I'd performed a sordid sex act I should have been too young to understand.

I thought about keeping up the pretence, about lying to Carly, too. She'd been really annoying ever since the first incident with Naseer, thinking she was really grown-up because she'd done something I hadn't, even though, deep down, we both knew she hadn't enjoyed it that much. But now that we were out of the boys' gaze, I couldn't be bothered fibbing anymore.

'Nah,' I replied. 'I don't fancy him.'

Carly giggled. 'I did it again,' she said. 'With Naseer. It's not that bad second time round. You kind of get to know what to do.'

Darkness was beginning to fall and it was getting cold. I pulled my jacket around me and looked at Carly in bemusement, but she didn't seem to notice. Just a few days ago, she'd been an innocent little girl with her hair in plaits, barely knowing the first thing about sex. Now she was boasting about giving out blow jobs. It was too much to take in.

The next night, as I called for Carly at her gran's, there was another surprise awaiting me. Gone was her trademark hairstyle; instead, her blonde hair was pushed into a high ponytail at the top of her head. I could tell she had done it herself, as the ponytail wasn't quite right – there were strands of hair escaping from the hair tie, and it was slightly off-centre – but I had to admit it was a big improvement on her childish plaits.

'Your hair . . .' I began.

'Oh yeah,' she said, dismissively. 'I was getting sick of the way my mum did it. I decided to do it myself. What do you think?'

'It's a bit messy at that side,' I answered, honestly. 'But it looks OK.'

She grinned. 'Thanks. Do you think I look older?'

'Yeah, a bit,' I said. 'It's better than the way it was.'

We walked our usual road towards the church but, as we ambled along the street, I suddenly heard shouting. The noise was coming from a group of Asian boys, standing across the street. I put my head down, as I assumed they weren't speaking to us, but suddenly I heard my name.

'Hey, Holly!' one boy said. 'Holly!'

I stopped so I could get a good look at him. He looked

around my age, maybe a year older. He was wearing an expensive jacket which looked a bit like Ali's. Before I could reply, he started making some kind of gesture I didn't really understand at first but I could feel my stomach twisting as I slowly figured out he was simulating a blow job.

'You gonna sort it for me, Holly? Eh? Gonna sort it?' his voice cracked a bit, like it was still breaking, but he didn't seem embarrassed.

His mates erupted into fits of laughter and my cheeks burned like never before. I wanted the ground to swallow me up.

'Fuck off,' I replied, with as much courage as I could muster. 'Don't be a dick.'

Mum would never have let me swear at home, and the words still felt funny as they rolled off my tongue.

'Come on, Holly,' another of the boys hollered. 'I heard you sorted it for Ali. Why can't you sort it for us?'

There was more laughter, and Carly started tugging on my sleeve.

'Why don't we just go over?' she said. 'It could be a laugh.'

'No, Carly,' I said, through gritted teeth. 'Leave it.'

'Hey, Holly,' the first boy shouted again. 'Who's your fat mate? Will she sort it for me instead?'

Carly looked at the ground, biting her lip. I couldn't help but feel sorry for her, especially as she'd tried so hard to make an effort by changing her hair. She was always being bullied for being fat and it must have been horrible.

'Just keep walking,' I told her. 'Ignore them. Don't say anything.'

We got to our bench and sat down as normal. Within

seconds, my phone began buzzing in my pocket. I took it out but, seeing it was a withheld number, I pressed cancel and put it away again.

'Who was that?' Carly asked.

'I dunno,' I said. 'I keep getting these weird prank calls but I don't answer.'

Before she could ask anything else, another group of lads was coming towards us. They looked Asian, too, but I assumed it was just a coincidence. I put my head down and waited for them to walk past us, but they broke into a chorus of wolf whistles and horrible sexual comments I couldn't make out over the noise. There were five of them. Again, they weren't much older than us, if at all, but I still felt really uncomfortable.

'Look!' one bellowed. 'It's her! The one who gave Ali a blow job. And her mate. She sucked off Naseer!'

Carly stood up and folded her arms. I had to admit that her behaviour since the first night with Naseer had been really odd. One minute she'd be her normal, babyish, slightly timid self, while the next she'd start acting really cocky and using swear words I'd never heard her say before.

'So what if I did?' she asked. 'Got a problem?'

'Carly!' I hissed, under my breath, not loud enough for the boys to hear. She ignored me. They were all hooting with laughter again.

'What you doing tonight then?' one of them asked. 'Fancy sorting me out, too?'

'Fuck off,' Carly said, as I stared at the ground. The boys carried on shouting things at us for a few minutes before they got bored and moved back along the street.

'Have Ali and Naseer been telling everyone we gave them blow jobs?' I asked Carly.

She shrugged. 'Well, someone must be spreading it around. At least I've actually done it. You didn't even suck his dick.'

The words, especially coming from Carly, still made me cringe.

'What's got into you, Carls?' I said. I deliberately used the nickname I'd made up for her when we were about nine, still playing football in the street and going home to our parents with skinned knees and mud-streaked tracksuits. 'Why are you suddenly swearing all the time and telling everyone you've given some guy a blow job? It's weird. You sound like an idiot.'

Anger flashed across her chubby face. 'Ha!' she retorted. 'You're just annoyed because I've done something you haven't. Are you annoyed because some lads are talking to me and not you?'

'No,' I answered, honestly. 'I just don't get why you're showing off so much. It's just a bit sad, really.'

Carly frowned. 'And you think you're cool, then? Just because your mum let you bleach your hair? Well, it looks shit. Your roots are coming through.'

We sat in stony silence for a few seconds, neither of us daring to speak. Eventually, Carly tugged at my arm.

'I'm sorry,' she said. Her voice was meek and babyish again. 'I like your hair. Your roots aren't coming through.'

'OK,' I said, still in a bit of a mood.

'Do you think I should bleach mine?'

Before I could answer, my phone started buzzing in my pocket again.

'Answer it,' Carly coaxed me. 'Don't you want to know who it is? I would.'

'I don't know . . .' I began, but curiosity had started to get the better of me and I did wonder who could possibly want to ring me so much. Hesitantly I pressed the answer button and held the phone to my ear.

'Holly!' the voice at the other end said. 'Holly!'

The caller had such a thick Pakistani accent that at first I thought he was calling me Kelly. He sounded old – much older than Ali, Naseer, Imran, or any of the other boys who'd shouted at Carly and me in the street. He also sounded really angry, like he was telling me off for something.

'Kelly?' I said, raising my eyebrows to Carly. 'I'm not Kelly.'

'Holly!' he repeated, in exasperation. 'Holly.'

I hung up. 'Just some old weirdo who thinks he's talking to someone called Kelly,' I said. 'Must be a mistake.'

But from then on, this mystery man started to call me morning, noon and night. It creeped me out so much that I started keeping my phone on silent all the time. I didn't want it going off constantly while I was in class, and I didn't want Mum to ask questions about why my phone was ringing all the time while I did my homework or ate my dinner.

My carefree nights walking through town with Carly were a thing of the past, too. Every night we'd get harassed by boys who'd heard the rumours, no doubt started by Ali and Naseer. Back then I thought it was nothing more than teenage bravado. I had no sense that these boys – boys the same age as us, who should have been at home doing their homework – were motivated by something far more sinister than a little bit of street cred.

'Sort it!' they'd always cry, as we shuffled past. 'Come on, Holly, sort it!'

'Sort it', I very quickly realised, was code for 'give us a blow job'. I tried to ignore them, but it was really hard as Carly seemed to get bolder by the day. She always shouted back at them, and I didn't understand why, because that meant we had to stand and talk to them for much longer than if we'd just ignored them. I guess she just liked the attention. I knew it pissed her off that they all made more sexual comments to me than they did to her. I suppose she just wanted to fit in and to feel like some lads found her attractive, which was a shame, really.

We still saw Ali and his mates some nights. Ali didn't ask me for a blow job again but all of the other boys did. It was like they were all gradually trying to grind me down, thinking that if enough of them asked me I'd eventually give in to one of them. Some people might wonder why I still went out at night, why I didn't make up some excuse to Carly, like telling her my mum had grounded me or something. It sounds a little sad, but one of the main reasons I kept going out was because I hoped I'd catch a glimpse of Imran. He was the only one of the boys who didn't hound me – in fact, he was really nice to me. Plus, there wasn't much else to do in Telford in the evenings apart from wander the streets, so at least it saved me from getting bored.

'Want to go for a walk?' Imran asked one night, as we were all sitting outside the church, near our usual bench.

I felt my stomach flutter a little. 'OK then.'

Carly was busy chatting to Ali and Naseer, and no doubt one of them would make her do something to them soon, anyway. I felt a bit bad leaving her alone with them, but I convinced myself she'd have done the same to me if someone as fit as Imran asked her to go for a walk.

We sat around the back of the church, but he didn't ask me to do anything to him. We just sat there and chatted about every-day things like school and our families. He was a year older than me; his dad was Pakistani and his mum was English. He insisted his dad was far less strict than lots of Muslims round our way. He owned a takeaway in town and Imran sometimes worked there at the weekends to help out.

'He doesn't give a shit what I do,' Imran laughed. 'He's always so busy with work and, you know, stuff. I could go out with any girl I liked and I bet he wouldn't say anything.'

'My mum's the same,' I said. 'She doesn't really bother what I do. She's always busy with work or my little sisters.'

This wasn't strictly true, of course. If Mum had an inkling of what these boys had asked Carly and me to do she'd have been horrified. But she'd just got a new job as a teaching assistant in a local school and she was frazzled running around after Lauren and Amy, who were both still toddlers. I had always behaved myself, more or less, and I'd never really given her any cause for concern. Despite what people were starting to say about me, I was always home before my curfew, so Mum had no reason to suspect I was slowly falling into the most unthinkable trap.

'Really?' he said. 'You're a good girl, though, I bet that's

why. My dad's not like Ali's or Naseer's. They're not supposed
to be going out with anyone. They're supposed to be waiting
until they get a wife.'

We both laughed.

'Not much chance of that,' I said.

Imran smiled at me and I had to catch my breath as he
slipped his arm around my neck. My body was stiff and rigid
and I felt really awkward and nervous. It took me a few minutes
before I allowed myself to lean into him. I was really worried
he'd try to kiss me, as I still wasn't sure what to do. I didn't
want it to be sloppy, like my kiss with Ryan had been, but that
was the only practice I'd had.

'You didn't really give Ali a blow job?' Imran said, as he
locked his fingers through mine. 'Did you?'

I blushed and looked at the ground. 'No,' I said, softly. 'But
everyone thinks I did.'

Imran started to laugh. 'I knew you didn't,' he said. 'I didn't
think a fit girl like you would just do that for no reason. Ali is
so full of shit sometimes. Anyway, maybe we should be getting
back.' He flashed me another smile, his brown eyes beaming.
'Don't worry, I won't tell anyone you sucked me off. In case
that's what you thought.'

'Thanks,' I said, weakly.

As we stood up, Imran took my hand again and looked into
my eyes. We stood there for a few seconds, staring at each
other, as if neither of us knew quite what to do. I expected him
to lean in for a kiss and my heart was hammering in my chest,
wondering if I could sort of improvise and kiss him like I knew
what I was doing.

Instead, he said, 'What's that noise? Is it your phone?'

My phone was on silent, as always, but it still vibrated when someone called and, if you listened carefully, you could hear a sort of low hum when it went off. I scrabbled in my pocket and noticed that it was another anonymous call. As quickly as I could, I cancelled it.

'Who's phoning you?' Imran asked.

'No one,' I said. 'Just a withheld number. Probably a prank call.'

Imran shrugged. 'I'm working in my dad's takeaway on Friday. It would be really nice if you could come down and say hello. Are you doing anything?'

My eyes lit up but I tried my best to sound cool as I replied. 'I'm not sure. I might come down, you know, if I'm free.'

Imran winked at me. 'Well, I hope you do.'

Friday came and I could barely concentrate in class because all I could think about was Imran. It was my first proper teenage crush, and every time his face popped into my head, I couldn't help but smile. I didn't tell any of my friends at school – they didn't know Imran, and I didn't think they would understand. Plus, I felt that if I said out loud how much I liked him, I might somehow jinx things between us.

I called for Carly at her gran's, as usual. She didn't know what I'd been planning, so I tried to keep it as casual as possible.

'So, um, want to walk into town?' I said.

She stared at me, a little confused. She was still wearing her hair in a high ponytail, but she'd obviously been practising, because it looked way better than her first couple of attempts. She'd also bought these ridiculous big hooped earrings, and she'd taken to wearing them every night.

'We always walk into town,' she said. 'Why are you even asking?'

'Oh, it's just . . .' I tried to pick my words carefully. 'Why don't we go past Imran's dad's takeaway? He's working. It could be a laugh.'

Carly shrugged. 'Won't that be a bit boring if he's just working?'

'We can just stop by,' I said. 'Just for five minutes.'

'OK,' she said. 'Do you like him?'

I blushed and let out a weak laugh. 'Nah, he's just my mate.'

The takeaway was down a side street, away from the main shops. It was near a few of the pubs and people would often come in for a curry or some pakora after a few pints. The first thing I noticed when I walked through the door was the pungent smell of the ghee, used to cook the curries. But when I looked up at the menu, there was loads of other food on sale too, like burgers and chips with cheese, and more Western dishes. The shop was really grubby. There were greasy fingerprints all across the counter and bits of stray food strewn on the floor. This surprised me, as Imran was always really well turned-out, wearing the best clothes. He was the only person behind the counter, which struck me as a little odd. He was only a year older than me and I assumed he'd have to be supervised by an adult.

'Hey!' he said, grinning as he saw us. He was shuffling a big wad of fat, uncooked chips into a fryer. They looked pale and unappetising. 'Thanks for coming.'

The shop was deserted, so Imran came out from behind the counter to talk to us. I could still smell his aftershave, but this time it was mixed with that distinctive greasy takeaway smell, which now makes me shudder. It was a bit awkward with Carly there, so we only stayed for five minutes, until a customer came in and he had to serve them.

'I'll see you next week,' he called, as we left, flashing me another of the smiles that made my stomach flutter.

I was in a bit of a daze as we ambled along the street, close to where we usually walked.

'You do like him!' Carly cried. 'You've gone all red!'

I could feel my face heating up again. 'I don't!' I protested. 'Carly, you can be mates with a guy without having to bloody suck them off.'

She didn't seem offended by my slight. 'Whatever. Hey, is that your phone ringing again?'

I fished my phone out of my jacket pocket and looked at the unknown number on the screen.

'It'll be that guy again,' I sighed. 'I wish he'd just leave me alone. I don't have a clue how he has my number or why he's phoning me.'

'Just answer,' Carly said. 'See what he wants.'

Against my better judgement, I pressed the phone to my ear. I was surprised to hear a different voice to the first one. The man on the other end still sounded Asian, and his English wasn't brilliant, but his voice was a bit deeper.

'Holly,' he said. 'Holly?'

'Yeah,' I replied. 'Who is it?'

He ignored my question. 'Come and meet me,' he said. 'Tomorrow.'

I didn't really know what to do, so I just hung up. I guess I had no idea of how serious it was that several older men seemed to have got hold of my phone number and were asking me to meet them. If a young girl came to me now and told me a similar story, alarm bells would ring and I'd be very worried for her safety. But back then I guess I was just naive. I didn't realise what was about to happen, so I pushed the phone calls to the back of my mind.

Instead, I spent my time daydreaming about Imran, and counting the hours until I might see him again. I didn't see him around town all weekend, and I was really disappointed, so when he was waiting by the bench on Monday evening, I was over the moon. I tried my hardest to stay calm and look cool, even when he asked if we could go round the back of the church for a walk. I wondered what Ali might say, considering he'd tried it on with me just a few weeks before, but he didn't seem bothered. He just laughed.

Thank God Imran is different, I thought. Thank God he's nothing like Ali.

Round the back of the church, Imran perched himself on a stone wall and motioned to me to join him. Again, he slipped his arm around my shoulder, but he didn't try to kiss me. I was a little confused. As much as the idea of snogging him made me nervous, I had expected him to at least have tried by now.

'Thanks for coming on Friday,' he said. 'It was really nice that you popped in to see me.'

I smiled. 'That's OK,' I replied.

His brown eyes fixed on me intently. 'I think you're really nice,' he said. 'I mean, you're fit and everything, but not just that. I like you.'

My heart skipped a beat. 'You like me?' I said.

'Yeah,' he grinned. 'I like you. I mean . . .' he trailed off for a few seconds. 'I want you to be my girlfriend.'

I didn't know what to say. Of course I was over the moon, but I was scared that if I opened my mouth no sound would come out, or I'd say something really embarrassing.

'Why have you gone quiet?' he laughed. I still said nothing, and his expression changed. As if on cue, he removed his arm from where it had been resting to around my waist. 'Oh. I get it. You don't like me like that?'

'No!' I answered, a little too quickly. 'I do.'

'You do?' he said, his brown eyes lighting up again. 'So you want to be my girlfriend then?'

I nodded. 'Mm-hmm,' was all I could manage to utter.

'Good,' he said, slipping his hand round my waist again. 'I'm glad.'

Neither of us said anything for a few seconds. Now Imran was my boyfriend, or at least that's what he'd said. It was what I'd wanted all along. But I'd never had a boyfriend before. What the hell was I supposed to do next?

'You know, maybe . . .' Imran began, before stopping. 'No, forget it. I couldn't ask you to do that.'

Desperate to please him, I urged him to go on.

'Well, maybe, if you want . . . but only if you want, and only because you're now my girlfriend, you could, you know . . .' he trailed off again.

'I could what?'

'You know, like, give me a blow job. But only if you want to. You don't have to.'

'Oh,' I replied, not sure what else to say. 'Right.'

'I know you're not like Carly,' he went on. 'I know you're not a slag. I know you wouldn't do it with just anyone. But it's different with me. You know you wouldn't be a slag if you did it with me, because I'm your boyfriend?'

I nodded, weakly. I'm not sure what was going through my head in those moments. All I could think was, this really fit guy wants me to be his girlfriend. Everyone at his school must fancy him like mad. If I don't do it now, will he think I'm a baby? Will he get bored and find another girl who will? Plus, it wasn't like I was being forced into it. Imran was nice. He said it was my choice, didn't he?

'Do you want to?' he said.

I bit my lip. 'OK, I'll do it. But you promise you don't think I'm a slag?'

He squeezed my shoulder. 'Of course not.'

But he was already unbuttoning his jeans, telling me to kneel down. I did as he said, as his jeans fell around his ankles. He gently took hold of my head, stroking my hair, as he placed it in his crotch.

It seemed to take an age before Imran had finished, but in reality the whole thing couldn't have lasted more than a few minutes. I didn't have a clue what to do, of course. I just kind of freestyled but I found the experience pretty disgusting. Occasionally, he'd push my head around a bit, or tell me what to do, but on the whole it seemed to work. As I was doing it, I remember thinking, isn't this strange? We haven't even kissed yet, but we're doing this. I was so eager to please, so desperate to be his girlfriend, that I didn't really question it. Naively, I just did as he said.

Finally, when it was over, I scrambled to my feet as he pulled his jeans back on. There were two muddy wet patches on the knees of my trousers, from where I'd been pressing into the damp ground. I looked intently at Imran, waiting for a reaction. I didn't know how these things worked. Was he supposed to say thanks? Tell me it was good? *Had* it been good? I just didn't know.

But, as he fastened the top button, he didn't say a word. He didn't even look at me. I stood there for a moment, in stunned silence, as he started to walk away.

'Imran,' I said, softly. I had to walk really fast to keep up with him. 'Imran!'

Ali and Naseer were standing round the front of the church with Carly. All three of them were looking at me. Suddenly, I felt a little bit sick.

'Sorted, mate!' Imran said. Ali and Naseer burst into a chorus of laughter. I could feel my whole body tense up and the bile was starting to rise in my throat as it slowly dawned on me what had happened.

Imran didn't want me to be his girlfriend. He'd wanted me to give him a blow job, just like Ali had. The only difference was he'd been much more careful, much more cunning. He was only fourteen, yet he'd callously manipulated me, slowly but surely, into thinking he liked me. As I stood behind him, knees still damp, there was a fleeting moment when I thought the tears might come, and I prayed they wouldn't. It was bad enough that I'd believed Imran when he'd said he wanted to be my boyfriend. It would be even worse if I started crying, right here in front of everyone.

I was surprised at how quickly I regained my composure. After a few seconds, I didn't feel like crying anymore. I just felt a little bit numb.

I didn't look at Imran as I grabbed Carly's arm and told her we were going. Behind me I could hear the boys, all three of them, making crude remarks, saying horrible sexual things about both of us. As much as I tried not to listen, it was Imran's voice I could hear above everyone else.

The walk home was a bit of a blur, and I think Carly knew I was in a mood because I didn't talk much. That night, as I climbed into bed, I had a strange feeling that something had changed forever. I still didn't cry, but there was a horrible, gnawing sensation in the pit of my stomach.

The only thought in my head was: you've done it. Now you really are a slag.

The next day, my phone rang again. This time I answered it, as if I was on autopilot. I didn't even think about it; I just did it. It was the older Pakistani man, the first one.

'Holly,' he said. 'Holly!'

His voice was still loud and aggressive and it still sounded like he was calling me Kelly. I held the phone a little away from my ear.

'Holly!' he repeated. 'You there?'

'Yeah, yeah,' I said. 'But who are you?'

'You call me Mr Khan,' he said sharply, in his broken English. 'I've seen you. At school. Now come meet me. Tomorrow. You come meet me. After school.'

'I don't know who you are,' I replied, bemused. 'How did you get my phone number?'

There was a short pause.

'The boy,' he said. 'The boy sold me number.'

'The boy?' I echoed. 'Sold you it? What? What do you mean?'

'Ali,' he said. 'Ali sold me number.' There was another brief pause, before he proudly added, 'And only cost me five pounds.'

4

Mr Khan

It transpired that Mr Khan didn't just have my phone number; he'd found out everything he could about me: my age, who my parents were, what school I went to, and even which way I walked home. I didn't know if he'd got his information directly from Ali or from someone else. One thing was for sure, though: he knew so much about me and I so little about him.

I didn't even have a clue what this mystery man looked like. It would be another few days before I'd find out, but he called me constantly. If I didn't answer, he'd get really mad and start phoning me at five-minute intervals. In the end, I figured it was best just to answer and keep him happy.

'You come meet me,' he'd say. 'After school.'

He never told me where to meet him, or what he looked like, so I assumed he was all talk. I guess I thought he'd soon get bored of me and stop calling. I didn't think I'd ever come face to face with him, not really.

So that's why I was a bit shocked when I was walking home from school as normal and a car began crawling along beside me. At first, I thought the driver was just parking up, or slowing down to drop someone off at the side of the road, so I kept walking. It was only after maybe a minute or so that I realised the car was following me. I stopped and squinted into the window, to get a good look at the man in the driver's seat. He had brown, leathery skin and piercing black eyes. I can still see those eyes now and I shudder when I think of them. Even in my youthful naivety I knew they had a look of pure evil about them. He was wearing traditional Asian clothes: a long white tunic, and matching loose-fitting trousers, but they looked a bit faded, as if he'd worn them loads of times and hadn't bothered to wash them.

He was a bit scruffy, really, so I was surprised when he opened his mouth to reveal a row of perfect, gleaming white teeth. He wasn't smiling, though. It was more of a grimace. I just stood there, staring at him for a few seconds, as he slowly rolled along the street. His eyes were firmly on me; he wasn't looking at the road. The street was built on a slight hill, so he didn't have to do much to keep the car moving. He was still staring at me as he wound down the window and pulled on the handbrake.

'Holly,' he said. 'Holly!'

My stomach twisted a little. I recognised the voice straight away, the thick accent with more than a hint of aggression. It was Mr Khan, my mystery caller.

I kept walking, picking up the pace a little, so he started moving again. 'Holly,' he said, again. 'Holly, I know your mum.'

I almost stopped in my tracks. If Mr Khan knew my mum, and he'd got my number from Ali, there was a good chance he'd know all the rumours about me. Now I'd actually given

Imran a blow job, it was much harder to deny everything. The abuse and catcalls were worse than ever. The word on the street was that Carly and I were dishing out blow jobs to pretty much everyone who asked us. I could just about deal with the vicious comments and gestures, but the idea of Mum finding out filled me with horror. She'd go absolutely spare.

I decided to pretend I hadn't heard and I was relieved when Mr Khan drove off. But within seconds he was calling my phone. I cancelled it, but almost immediately he started calling again, and again, like he had my number on redial. I turned the corner to see him sitting in his little car at the side of the street, eyes boring into me.

'Get in,' he ordered me.

For a moment, I was frozen to the spot but, after a few seconds, I did as I was told. Some people might think this seems odd. Who in their right mind would willingly get into a strange man's car, especially a strange man who has been hounding you with phone calls after apparently buying your number for a fiver? But unless you've been groomed as a child, you'll probably never understand. Mr Khan hadn't said much to me, but I already knew he was scary – really scary. He knew so much about me that he'd find me eventually, even if I said no this time. He'd be much angrier if I just walked away, so it was easier to do as I was told. Plus, he said he knew Mum, and I was terrified he'd tell her all the rumours about me if I didn't do as he said.

I reached for the door on the passenger's side, but he had already pushed the seat back.

'No, no,' he barked. 'You go there. Lie down!'

I was a bit confused at first, but he pushed me onto the back seat and made me lie flat.

'Now no one can see,' he explained. He was so matter-of-fact it almost seemed normal, as he drove away and I lay flat on my stomach, staring at the grubby interior of his car and wondering what the hell was going on. It sounds crazy, but all I could think was, what if the police stop us and I haven't got a seatbelt on? I'll be in huge trouble and Mum will be so mad. As strange as it sounds, it didn't occur to me that the police should probably have been more concerned that Mr Khan was driving around Telford with a fourteen-year-old girl hidden in the back of his car, still wearing her school uniform.

In the end, he drove for ten, maybe fifteen minutes. I didn't dare look up, but I could feel the car slowing down, going over lumps and bumps, as if we weren't driving on a proper road. Eventually, he slowed to a stop.

'You can get out,' he said, still in the same, aggressive tone. I sat up and I recognised my surroundings immediately. We were at the end of a dirt track in the woods near a place called Wellington, where Mum would often take us to gather nuts and conkers.

I was scared. It was still light outside but, if something happened, what would I do? I could try screaming for help but I couldn't see anyone for miles around. The place looked completely deserted. I swallowed hard.

It's fine, I told myself, just do as he says and it will all be fine. He'll drop you back home and you can just forget this.

Mr Khan motioned to me to come and sit next to him in the passenger seat, now that we were away from the gaze of mums on the school run. I could feel two little beads of sweat forming on the back of my neck as I obliged, and he started to speak. His English was really poor, so I couldn't really make out anything he was saying. I just nodded politely, hoping he'd soon stop talking and take me home.

'Your mum,' he said. 'She is teacher?'

I nodded. 'Yeah, well, kind of.'

'My daughter . . . at her school,' he said. Again, he added, 'I know your mum.'

I was still confused. 'But how do you know that's my mum?' I asked him.

He ignored me, and started speaking about something else. I had to strain my ears and listen to every word really carefully, but I still didn't understand what he was trying to say.

'How did you know where I was going to be?' I went on. 'Who told you what school I was at?'

He never did answer my question. We sat in silence for a few more minutes, before he told me to get into the back of the car again. I did as he said, lying flat just like before. He sped off and, after about ten minutes, he screeched to a halt. I sat up slowly and saw that we were on the road where he'd picked me up. He motioned to me to lie back down again and I did as he indicated.

Out of the corner of my eye, I could see that he had pulled a wad of receipts out of his top pocket. He started leafing through them, and eventually he handed me a grubby-looking ten-pound note.

'For you,' he said.

Still hidden away on the back seat, I reached out and took it from him, feeling confused but pleased. I'd been scared when he'd picked me up, there was no doubt about that. He seemed like a really aggressive man and I'd spent most of the journey wondering if he would hurt me. But he'd now taken me back to where he'd found me without doing anything – and he'd given me a tenner, just like that. Maybe he wasn't so bad after all.

'You need anything, you call me,' he said, slowly. 'OK?'

'Need anything?' I echoed, feeling a little bemused.

'You know,' he barked. 'Food. Money. A lift. Money for phone.'

He motioned for me to sit up and get out of the car, so I did, as quickly as I could, without another word. As he drove off, I dialled Carly's number on my phone and waited for her to answer.

'Come and meet me by the phone box,' I told her. 'You know that guy who phones me all the time? He just gave me a tenner. For nothing.'

'Really?' Carly gasped. 'That's amazing!'

Within minutes she'd arrived, and we'd walked to a petrol station about half a mile away, where we stocked up on crisps, juice and sweets. Neither of us got much pocket money, so having a bit of cash was amazing – although we couldn't really think of what to spend it on.

'I can't believe he gave you money for nothing,' Carly said. 'Why would he do that?'

I shrugged. 'Dunno.'

'What's he like?' she said.

'Creepy,' I replied. 'Like, proper weird. But still, he gave me money, didn't he?'

We both laughed.

'Do you think he'll try to pick you up again?' she asked, taking a handful of crisps.

'Not sure,' I said. 'He told me I could phone him whenever I wanted anything, though.'

Carly's eyes widened. 'Anything?'

'Well, you know, like phone credit and stuff,' I said.

I still felt uneasy about Mr Khan, but I can't lie. Like most teenagers, I liked the idea of getting something for nothing, although I didn't understand why a stranger would want to give me money or buy me things without expecting anything in return. Especially as Mr Khan didn't seem kind or generous, but scary and threatening.

Still, when he stopped me on the way home from school the next night, I agreed to get into the car. For the next couple of weeks he'd drive me out to a secluded spot – sometimes the woods where we'd collected conkers, sometimes the foot of the Wrekin – and we'd just sit in the car for about a quarter of an hour before he'd take me back to the road he'd found me on. He didn't attempt to do anything to me, but sometimes he'd give me this look which would send shivers down my spine. I had a bad feeling about him, but I told myself I was being paranoid, as he was still buying me things and giving me money. Sometimes he'd give me a tenner, like he had on the first afternoon. Other times he'd stop at a takeaway and buy me loads of food. There would be so much of it that I'd have enough to share with Carly, when he dropped me off on the road near my school.

'This guy is such a mug,' Carly giggled. 'He gives you so much stuff for free!'

'I'm not complaining,' I laughed, as we tucked into our curry and naan bread. We never had takeaway at home. Mum didn't see the point. She had five kids to feed, after all, and if we asked if we could phone for a curry, she'd tell us it was a waste of money.

'What's the point in spending twenty quid on a curry?' she'd say. 'I can get one in Iceland for a fiver and it'll do us all just fine.'

At that moment, my phone started buzzing. I answered it and the voice on the other end was that of another Asian man. He sounded a bit like Mr Khan, only slightly younger and his English was even worse.

'Meet me,' was all he'd say, in a strong Pakistani accent. 'Meet me.'

I hung up, feeling a little embarrassed. When I explained the call to Carly, she was confused, too. It was one thing meeting one older man and him giving me money. It was quite another if I started to meet loads of them. I imagined what Mum would say if she found all the numbers in my phone. I can't imagine she'd have been too impressed.

But ever since Imran had rejected me, my self-esteem had plummeted. I'd given him a blow job before we'd even kissed. Sure, I'd liked him, but didn't that make me a slag? By that point, I had it in my head that maybe I deserved to have my phone number passed around lots of sleazy older men. Maybe I should just have been grateful none of them had laid a finger on me, that they actually wanted to give me gifts and money for simply sitting in a car for a bit before I went home to do my homework.

Plus, it was much better than just hanging around town with Carly. We still spent loads of time together, but we'd taken to avoiding our usual spot by the bench at the church because the younger boys were getting worse and worse. They called us names we didn't even understand and, sometimes, they'd grab us as we walked along the road, demanding a blow job. Even Carly had started to get sick of it, though she still sometimes wanted to meet up with Ali and his mates. I was less keen, because I wanted to avoid Imran like the plague. I hadn't really seen him since that night when he'd humiliated me, and I was scared of what he might say if we bumped into him.

One night, though, I was walking past the church on the way home from Carly's, when a car whizzed past me. Its windows were completely blacked out, so I couldn't see who was inside. The thud of the bass from the stereo reverberated across the pavement, as the car spun round the roundabout and drove back the way it had come. It was a few seconds before it slowed to a stop, right next to me.

The driver stuck his head out, and the first thing that struck me was how ugly he was. His face was dominated by two huge protruding front teeth. They had a massive gap between them and were a weird orange colour, like they hadn't been brushed in months.

'Holly,' he said. His Pakistani accent sounded oddly familiar. Within a few seconds, I realised he was the man with the really bad English who had been phoning me, just like Mr Khan had.

His friend leaned over and popped his head out of the window. He looked Asian, too, but spoke with an English accent.

'Get in,' he told me.

He didn't seem overly threatening, so I did as he said. It sounds mental, of course, and as an adult I'm aware that anything could have happened to me, just as it could have with Mr Khan on the dirt track. But back then, walking home alone meant running the gauntlet of the teenage boys and their comments and catcalls without even Carly and her increasingly big mouth to protect me. Without giving it much thought, I jumped in.

The men looked like they were in their late twenties or early thirties. The one in the passenger seat told me his friend had just come to England from Pakistan because he'd had an arranged marriage with a girl who worked in the big Tesco in Telford. Neither told me their names.

The English friend and I made a bit of small talk for a few minutes but we soon ran out of things to say. I could sense that the man with the bad English was driving towards the Wrekin, and I felt a bit panicky because it's really spooky at night. There are no lights in the car park and it's really, really dark. When we got there, his friend told me to get out.

What happened next was really weird.

I opened the door and the night air hit my face. I could feel my cheeks reddening in the biting cold, as I pulled my denim jacket around me.

A little sheepishly, the man with the bad English gestured to the other side of the car park and led me there. He took me behind some trees and I started to feel a little light-headed, wondering what I'd got myself into and praying he wouldn't demand a blow job, because I really didn't want to give him one.

We stood in silence, facing each other, for what seemed like an eternity. He gave me a weak half-grin, flashing his terrible teeth. In that moment, I really did feel quite sorry for him. The only thought in my head was: it's a shame for him, really. He looks so much like a beaver.

Once I'd made the comparison, I could never think of him as anything but 'Beaver', as cruel as it sounded. He had no idea of my train of thought as he stood looking at me, as if he expected me to say or do something.

'You all right there?' I asked, breaking the long silence.

He nodded. 'Look,' he began. 'At my dick.'

He dropped his trousers. The cool night air had made the thick dark hair on his legs stand on end. Next came his boxers, as I watched with a mix of horror and bemusement, half-expecting what was coming next and wondering if I'd have any choice in the matter.

But after a few seconds he lifted his boxers again. He looked bashful as he stepped back into his trousers, fastening the button at the top, then he simply motioned for me to go back to the car. After that, they dropped me at the end of my road and I walked back into the house like nothing had happened.

Mum didn't really notice anything because Mr Khan and the other men never kept me out late or for very long. I always told her I was with Carly or one of my school friends, and she never questioned me. I became very secretive very quickly, though. My phone was glued to my hand and I'd never leave it lying around the house, because I was terrified Mr Khan or Beaver or someone else would ring and Mum would pick it up out of curiosity.

'Can't you go five minutes without looking at that thing?' Mum would ask, occasionally, but I'd just grunt in typical teenage fashion. Most kids my age spent hours on their phones and she had no reason to suspect anything untoward.

I quickly became concerned about the money from Mr Khan, too. It was only a tenner here and there, but I worried what Mum would say if she found notes in my purse. I usually only had a couple of quid on me for my lunch. I couldn't think of a decent excuse for having all this cash, so I hid it all under a floorboard in my room.

About three weeks after Mr Khan had first picked me up, I went to my friend Jenny's house after school, which meant I hadn't walked home my usual way. I could feel my phone vibrating in my pocket and Mr Khan's number was flashing up on the screen. When I answered he started screaming and swearing at me, cursing me for not walking home via my normal route. I actually felt a little shaken – I didn't think I'd done anything wrong, as we'd never made any formal plans to meet. He just always seemed to know where I was, and he'd always pick me up in the same spot. But then I started to feel guilty. He'd given me all these things and, so far, expected nothing in return. Maybe he was right to be angry that I wasn't there.

I hung up quickly, though. None of my school friends knew about this secret arrangement we had, and I didn't want to tell them because, deep down, I knew it was weird. I was already being called a slag by lots of boys in the street, but most of them went to Carly's school, so my classmates had no idea of my reputation. And I was in no rush for them to find out.

'Who was that?' asked Jenny.

'Oh, wrong number,' I mumbled, and changed the subject. Thankfully, she didn't ask any more questions.

For the next few hours, Mr Khan hounded me with phone calls. I ignored several, before answering one call as I walked home from Jenny's. He screamed at me again, and I hung up, but seconds later he was calling me once more. This went on for ages, and he sounded angrier and angrier as the clock ticked on. I was torn between answering and listening to his tirade of abuse and ignoring him, which seemed to wind him up even more. As I went to bed that evening, I felt a knot of dread twist in my stomach, like something really bad was about to happen.

Of course, I made sure I walked home the usual way the next evening. I was a bit scared of Mr Khan, but at the same time I also couldn't be bothered with the hassle if I didn't go for a drive with him. Anyway, he'd only want to sit in the car with me for a bit then buy me some food from the takeaway, before taking me home. How bad could it be?

As always, he pulled up at the side of the road and bundled me into the back. But this time he was just a little more forceful than usual as he pushed me through the door, and I felt my heart beat a little faster. I glanced up and, as his eyes bored into me, I sensed something had changed.

As soon as he turned the key in the ignition, he started to shout at me. I couldn't understand some of what he was saying, as his English was so bad, but I got the gist of it. He was calling me lots of names, some in his own language, and telling me I had to do what he said and I was never to go home a different way again.

This time, he drove to the end of a dirt track a few miles out of town. As always, he ordered me into the front seat but, this time, he rubbed his hand on my thigh. I tensed as he ran his cold hand up and down my leg, slowly pushing up my school skirt. Before I could protest, he was leaning towards me with his mouth open. Although he had perfect teeth, his breath was horrendous, like he hadn't brushed them in ages. His black moustache bristled against my face as I recoiled in horror.

'Get off me!' I shouted instinctively, as I drew away.

I felt completely and utterly disgusted, but I also felt stupid, too. Of course Mr Khan wanted something in return for the money and the takeaways. How could I have been so naive? I barely had time to hold this thought in my head, before he lurched towards me and tried to kiss me again.

'No!' I said, as firmly as I could. 'Stop it!'

He looked at me, fury burning in his piercing, evil eyes. For a moment, he was deathly silent. I held my breath, waiting for him to fly into a rage. I even wondered if he might hit me.

But he calmly turned the key in the ignition and said: 'Out.'

'Out?' I repeated. 'But we're in the middle of nowhere.'

'Out,' he said, again. Finally, he raised his voice. 'Get out!'

He prodded my arm, as I picked up my school bag and scrambled out of the car onto the dirt track. Without another word, he turned the car round and sped off into the distance. I stood there in disbelief for a few seconds, expecting him to come back, but that wasn't going to happen. Eventually I realised I had no choice but to start walking home. It was only a few miles out of town but the sun was starting to set and I felt a little scared as I trudged through the woodland. If something happened to me, who would know to look for me here?

When I finally got home, Mum was dishing out dinner as she balanced Amy on her hip.

'Where have you been?' she asked. 'You're a bit late.'

'Just with Carly,' I lied. 'I'm here now.'

She didn't ask any more questions, and I was relieved.

From then on, I knew things were very different. I still went to school and, to my teachers, I suppose I looked like a normal pupil. I'd overcome the hurdles I'd faced at primary and my grades were above average. Even with my mild dyslexia, I did quite well in English and I didn't really mind IT, either. Where I really excelled was in travel and tourism, my favourite subject, and I still told people I wanted to be an air hostess.

But I was already becoming a very different person to the little girl who'd sat on the plane to Majorca, wide-eyed and eager to explore the world.

I guess I probably didn't stick out much to my teachers. I wasn't top of the class, or the teacher's pet, but neither did I disrupt the class or refuse to do my homework, so I wasn't loads of trouble, either. My school uniform was always clean and I came from a good home. My parents had jobs and they fed me and clothed me and turned up to parents' night. How was anyone to know I was being slowly sucked into a horrible, depraved world that was beyond my control?

It sounds bad, but there were other girls my age in Telford who probably caused the teachers more of a headache, although usually through no fault of their own. Most of them were in care, or at least had a social worker. I'd never met a social worker in my life and Mum would have been horrified if it had even been suggested that social services should get involved with our family. Surely if anyone was at risk from predatory older men it was those girls from troubled backgrounds, not me.

But every night, when the school bell rang, I knew it was time to meet Mr Khan. Even if I was more than a couple of minutes late, he'd phone and shout at me. He really, really scared me – much more than he had done before. Sometimes we'd just sit in the car and he wouldn't do anything, but other times he'd kiss me and it was horrible but I felt like I had to oblige because I didn't want him to dump me in some godforsaken spot in the middle of nowhere.

I'd grimace as he forced his tongue down my throat and the harshness of his six o'clock shadow scratched my face. I held my nose as much as I could, so I didn't have to smell his horrible odour – sweat mixed with cheap soap and unclean clothes. I never saw him wear anything but his white tunic and drawstring trousers and I wondered if he'd ever washed them.

I didn't really tell Carly about the kisses. I don't think I told anyone, not at first. I already felt like a slag because of everything that had happened with the boys my own age. To admit, out loud, that a man who was old enough to be my dad was driving me to the middle of nowhere and sticking his tongue down my throat in exchange for a tenner or a portion of chips and a naan bread made me feel even more cheap and worthless.

One evening, after he'd taken me to the foot of the Wrekin,

I was walking through town with Carly when we saw Ali from afar. He was surrounded by a group of lads.

'Hey, Holly!' he shouted. 'Meet me in ten minutes, eh? Will you sort it?'

I tried to tell him to fuck off, but his mates started shouting that I was a slag and making noises and gestures. Eventually Carly and I decided to sit on a bench in an alleyway a few streets along, just to get away. But there was no escaping these boys, not for any length of time. Before long, two Asian lads from her school had spotted us and plonked themselves down next to us. I rolled my eyes.

'All right, Carly,' the first said. 'Who's your mate?'

'Her name's Holly,' Carly replied.

'Holly,' he said. 'Oh yeah. I've heard about you.'

The lads were a bit of a pain, but they weren't quite as rude as Ali, so I just put up with them. I knew what they wanted because they kept dropping hints, but I hoped they'd go away eventually.

All of a sudden, I was aware of an older Asian man walking towards me. He was really scruffy, with stubble on his face and greying hair. He wasn't dressed in traditional clothes like Mr Khan. He had black jeans on, and a long black coat that came to his knees. He started talking to the lads we were with.

'Hey, Kev!' one said. 'This is Holly.'

The man span round to look at me. Something about his dark eyes looked oddly familiar, which was weird because I'd never seen him in my life before. I could feel his gaze travelling from my face to my still-developing breasts, lingering on my body for a few seconds before he spoke.

'Oh yeah,' he replied, with a nod of recognition. 'I've heard about all the stuff you get up to.'

My face burned. For what seemed like the hundredth time in the last few months, I asked the dreaded question: 'How do you know who I am?'

He laughed. 'Because I just do. Most people know who you are, love.'

I wished the ground would swallow me up, as I gazed at him, bemused.

'You know what,' he said. 'If you're going to do all of that stuff, you might as well get paid for it. I can sort you out.'

I still wasn't really following. 'What do you mean?'

'I know what you've been up to,' he said again. 'No point in trying to fool me. But why are you doing all this for free? You could be making a fortune. Do you know Lily Brown?'

I nodded slowly. 'I know who she is, kind of. She's at my school but she's older than me.'

'Well, let me tell you this. Lily Brown has made £17,000 doing what you do. She's going to get driving lessons and everything with the money. All I'm saying is, don't give it away for free like you're doing now. Think about it.'

My mouth hung open, as he walked away with his hands in his pockets.

'Who the hell is that?' I asked.

'Oh, his name's Kev,' one said. 'He's Imran's dad. He's a pimp.'

5

Kev

I had an idea what a pimp was. I knew it was something to do with selling women for sex, but I somehow imagined a suave man in a purple velvet suit with a big cane, like something you'd see in a film. I didn't think of a scruffy guy who owned a downmarket takeaway in Telford.

I also wondered why they called him Kev. Although he didn't dress like Mr Khan and some of the other Asian men I saw around town, he was obviously Pakistani. His skin was much darker than even Imran's, and his West Midlands accent had a faint foreign twang. But why didn't he use his real name? It struck me as more than a bit odd.

Imran had told me he had an English mum, and that's why he looked a bit different to Ali and Naseer. The cogs turned in my brain, as I realised this meant Kev was living with someone outside of his faith, which was quite unusual in his community.

As Carly chatted to the lads, I thought about Imran and how he'd claimed his dad didn't give a shit what he did, while other Asian boys were kept on a short leash. Had Imran told his dad about what I'd done? It seemed absurd, but the thought played on my mind and it made me feel a bit sick. In the end I convinced myself he must have been a friend of someone like Beaver or Mr Khan. But there were so many people spreading rumours about me, he could have heard them from countless sources.

And, if truth be told, I kept thinking about what he'd said about Lily Brown and the £17,000. I wondered what she'd had to do for it. Did she have to have sex with men? I couldn't help but think what I could do with all of that money. I'd considered myself rich when Mr Khan handed me a tenner because I could buy some crisps and fizzy drinks. £17,000 was beyond my wildest dreams. I imagined being able to get driving lessons and a really nice car. I didn't have any idea how much houses cost, but I fantasised I'd be able to buy one of those, too, when I was old enough, if I started saving now.

All the while, Kev's words rang in my head: 'If you're going to do all the stuff you do, you might as well get paid for it.'

Of course, I hadn't really done much. I'd given Imran the blow job and I'd let Mr Khan rub my thighs and stick his tongue down my throat a few times. I say I'd let him, but I didn't really feel I had an option. The problem was, everyone thought I was a slag. The rumours about me were ten times more outrageous than the reality. No matter what I did, grown men persistently called me, asking to meet me, and boys my own age gestured to me on the street, demanding blow jobs. Maybe, just maybe, if people were going to say all of these horrible things about me, I deserved something in return.

'What would you do with £17,000?' I asked Carly, as we approached her front door.

'Oh, my God, I dunno,' she said. 'Do you think that guy was being serious about Lily Brown?'

I shrugged. 'Could be. Anyway, night.'

The whole of the next day I thought about Kev and what he'd said. His words were a bit like a poison, slowly seeping into my brain. I had no idea how much I was already being manipulated and abused by various different men. I just hated being called a slag, but here was someone who claimed he could make it worth my while.

I'd never seen Kev around before, and he'd never phoned me like Mr Khan or Beaver or the others, so I assumed it might be weeks or months before I bumped into him again. I could have just walked into the takeaway, but I didn't want to see Imran.

As chance would have it – or maybe it wasn't chance at all – I met Kev again a few days later. Mr Khan had picked me up as usual after school and driven me into the woods. He hadn't kept me long, just enough to grope my legs under my school skirt and shove his horrible tongue down my throat. When I'd had my sloppy first kiss at the disco with Ryan, I couldn't imagine anything worse, but at least Ryan had brushed his teeth. The foul taste of Mr Khan's unclean mouth, and the thought of his wiry moustache on my lips, is still enough to make me gag, even today.

Kev was standing by a phone box on the main road, the one where I often met Carly after Mr Khan dropped me home.

'Holly,' he said. 'All right?'

I nodded. 'Yeah, yeah. You?'

'Yeah,' he said. 'Good. What are you up to?'

I shrugged. 'Just heading home from school.'

Kev looked at his watch and laughed. 'School finished ages ago. Where have you been?' He had a weird glint in his eye. 'Up to no good, eh?'

I didn't answer.

'Hey,' he said. 'You know what I was saying to you the other night? About Lily Brown?'

My guard dropped a little. 'Does she really have all that money?'

Kev nodded. 'She sure does. It's all in the bank. Why don't you think about it, eh? Easy money, it really is.'

'What would I, you know, have to do?' I asked. 'Like, to get the £17,000?'

The corners of Kev's mouth twitched a little. 'Well, you'd have to have sex with someone, wouldn't you?'

Even in my naivety, I'd guessed all along that this was what he'd want me to do. I always imagined losing my virginity would be years away, maybe with a first boyfriend that I really loved. I tried to think about what the men Kev would have lined up for me would be like. I didn't have a clue about sex. What was I supposed to do? How was I supposed to act? Would it be sore? Maybe I'd just have to close my eyes and think about what I could do with the money.

'Don't worry,' Kev laughed. 'You can think about it. But if you do want to do it, you'll have to pass a test first.'

Now, I can see Kev was playing a long game but at the time it was like he was giving me some kind of opportunity. Over the next few weeks, I saw him most nights, mainly when I'd just been dropped off by Mr Khan. It sounds absurd, two middle-aged men passing me around like a piece of meat, but by then I think I was so brainwashed it just seemed normal. When I was with Kev, we'd just talk at first. Sometimes, we'd talk about normal things but sometimes he'd mention Lily and the other girls who worked for him and all the things they'd bought for themselves with the money they'd got. He didn't pressure me, not really. He just slowly and calmly fed me all this information. He never talked about the men, only the money.

He also kept mentioning Imran to me, teasing me and asking me if I fancied him. I'd always try to change the subject, but he was having none of it.

'You know I can set you up with him,' he said. 'If you like him.'

My face burned as I mumbled that, really, it was OK. I wondered again if Imran had told him what we'd done, or even that we'd come into the takeaway one night to visit while he'd been working. I wanted just to forget about Imran, but now I see that that he too was a sick pawn in Kev's game: a handsome teenage son; just another carrot to dangle in front of me so I'd think a little bit more about doing what he wanted.

One evening he took me back to his house and I quickly discovered he had a rather strange domestic set-up. He was married, but not to Imran's mum. His wife was Pakistani, just like him, but they lived apart. They had children together, but they were grown up, a few years older than Imran and his siblings. Ever dutiful, his wife cooked his dinner every night and brought it round to him in a little dish, even though he'd chosen to leave her for Imran's mum. To me, it seemed completely mental, like Mum driving round to Dad's every night with leftovers from our tea, even though they'd split up years ago and she was happy with Phil.

The family home was on a nondescript street in Telford, a semi-detached ex-council house indistinguishable from all the others around it. I pushed open the black iron gate and walked down the path to the front door, following as Kev led the way. When he opened the door, the first thing I caught sight of was Imran's little sister standing at the top of the stairs, outside her mum's bedroom, as if she was standing guard. She was younger than me, ten, maybe eleven, with impish black eyes and a startled look on her face.

'Liz isn't very well,' Kev explained.

On my later visits to the house, I'd discover that Liz had multiple sclerosis and often was too weak to get out of bed. She had not one daughter but two, both a few years younger than me, but I'd soon come to realise that they cared for her pretty much round the clock, while Imran and his brother Farooq did as they pleased.

The younger sister stood at the top of the stairs – Ayesha, as I'd soon discover she was called – gave me a long, shy look, as if she didn't quite know what to say. The older sister, Nadia, was soon behind her, staring at me equally wide-eyed. After a few moments, they both retreated back into the bedroom, closing the door without a word to either their dad or me. I could just about make out the sound of them whispering as they closed the door.

Kev ushered me into the living room. It looked like any front room in any street in Telford. The carpet was an unremarkable cream colour, as were the walls, and the shelves were full of the kids' faces beaming from school pictures. For a moment, it almost seemed a bit too normal.

But, of course, this house wasn't normal at all.

It was a few seconds before I became aware of the low moans coming from the corner of the room. My eyes darted from Imran's smiling school picture – conventional as can be – to the huge flat-screen television on the wall. As the image on the screen slid into focus, it was all I could do not to gasp in dismay. A blonde woman with huge fake breasts was writhing around on top of a balding, middle-aged man, and they were both making all sorts of noises. I'd never seen two people having sex before, and I'd always wondered what it might look like, but my curiosity quickly gave way to a mixture of horror and embarrassment as I became aware of the figure in the corner.

In the armchair sat Farooq – twelve-year-old Farooq – with his trousers and pants around his ankles, masturbating furiously as he watched this filthy porn film. I'd never seen anything like it in my life, and I clasped my hands to my face in horror as I tried not to look at the two figures jiggling around on the screen. The blonde woman's moans were getting faster, and more high-pitched, as she tossed her huge mane of hair around. She was completely naked, apart from her stiletto heels. My face was scarlet and I wanted to look anywhere but at the screen, but that meant I couldn't avoid watching Farooq openly pleasuring himself as his dad and I looked on.

I stared at both of them, as Farooq's eyes landed on us. I expected him to recoil in horror, to pull his trousers up and run off, just about dying of shame. But he was completely unde-terred and interested in nothing but the titillation onscreen. My eyes travelled from Kev to Farooq to Kev again, with a mixture of shock and amazement. For a moment I considered that Kev might be as shocked as I was. Despite what he did and how he made his money, he surely didn't allow his sons to do that in full view of visitors and anyone passing by outside, who might just happen to look in the window and see him. Did he?

But Kev didn't even move to turn the porn film off. He simply burst into uproarious laughter and slapped Farooq round the back of the head.

'You dirty bastard!' he said. 'What's he like?'

I'd fixed my eyes on a spot on the carpet, hoping that when I looked up this weird and disgusting spectacle would all be over but, when I raised my eyes, Farooq was still going, his moans becoming louder and more frequent. Kev didn't even bat an eyelid. He was more interested in the wad of cash he'd pulled from his pocket, which he was counting out meticulously, note by note.

All I could think was: why on earth is Farooq wanking in front of his *dad*? And why is his dad *letting* him?

I continued to stare at the ground as the moans continued. It was the smallest of snapshots into Imran's family life but, in five minutes, I'd learned so much about the kind of home he came from. It almost made me laugh, thinking of my dad and how he'd react in a situation like that. He'd have been bloody horrified, and no wonder! Most parents would, and most teenagers wouldn't dream of doing it in front of their dad in the first place. But Farooq wasn't like most teenagers, and Kev certainly wasn't like most parents.

Eventually Farooq's moans stopped and he exhaled loudly.

A smug, satisfied grin spread across his face. Instinctively, I turned away.

'You going to say hello to Holly now you've finished?' Kev chuckled, like he'd been playing his PlayStation, or texting on his phone.

Farooq gave me a sullen: 'All right.'

I nodded back, still stunned. For once, I was glad he didn't have the manners to shake my hand.

Imran and Farooq seemed so different. Imran had been so manipulative, cunning beyond his years, yet Farooq appeared to have absolutely no social graces or concept of what was acceptable behaviour. But ultimately they'd wanted the same thing – easy sexual gratification without any emotion or thought for anyone they embarrassed or hurt in order to get it. I found myself looking from father to son again and wondering: where have they learned to behave like this?

Kev didn't give me much time to contemplate the whole sordid spectacle because, shortly afterwards, he took me home. It had been a largely pointless visit and I wasn't sure why he'd brought me there, but I didn't say anything.

'It's pizza for tea,' Mum said, as I pushed open the door. Amy and Lauren were sitting on the living-room floor, toys strewn around them, watching *The Powerpuff Girls* on television.

'Right,' I replied. 'Cool.'

The incredible scene I'd just witnessed was still flashing through my mind, as if it was on a loop. Now I was back in my own very normal living room, it seemed all the more surreal. Amy caught sight of me out of the corner of her eye and bounded up to give me a hug, handing me her doll in the process.

'How's Carly?' Mum asked, as she fiddled with the timer on the oven.

'Fine,' I said.

'Have you done your homework?' she continued. 'Don't leave it too late to finish it or you'll be tired for school tomorrow.'

Being tired for school was the last thing I could think about. I was still so overwhelmed and astounded by what I'd just seen. As Amy tugged at my hand and led me to her toy box, I momentarily asked myself if I'd somehow imagined it all.

Kev was a lot different from Mr Khan, in that he didn't try to hide me away. He was quite brazen. In those first few weeks he'd sit with me in the front seat of the car with no concern for who might see. His back seat was often piled high with take-away food to deliver, and sometimes he'd leave me sitting there while he called at houses on the way back to Mum's, before dropping me at the end of the road. Sometimes he'd give me free food, just like Mr Khan had, but there was no money. Not yet.

It was almost a month before he properly mentioned it again. I'd just jumped into his car when he casually brought up Lily and the test, asking had I decided, did I want to make some easy money?

I couldn't lie. I did. Otherwise I'd never have kept seeing him and going to his weird house.

'I mean,' Kev laughed. 'All the names they call you. I've

heard them. You might as well make it worth your while. You're doing all of this anyway, aren't you?'

I didn't know what the right answer was, so I stayed silent.

'Might as well make some money,' Kev went on. 'And I can make you good money.'

'OK,' I said.

Kev turned the key in the ignition and his car spluttered into life. 'If, of course, you pass my test.'

I said nothing as he sped off and the car chugged through the residential streets of Telford until gradually we left them behind and the Wrekin grew closer and closer. Kev swung into the car park at the foot, where I'd been so many times with Mum and, lately, with Mr Khan.

Night was beginning to fall, although it was just past five o'clock, and there wasn't a soul for miles around. Suddenly Kev had stopped talking and the car park was eerily quiet. I could feel my pulse quickening, just slightly, wondering what was about to happen next. Kev laid his hand on my thigh, pushing my school skirt up ever so slightly, a bit like the way Mr Khan had done, but it felt far more clinical. There was no hint of desire, or even of aggression. Kev had a calculating look in his eyes as he stroked my leg and furrowed his brow, like I was a product in a shop window and he was trying to estimate my value.

'Get in the back,' he said.

Wordlessly, I did as he said. He followed me and threw open the door.

'OK,' he said, after a few seconds. 'I'm going to start touching you. And you're going to start making sex noises.'

I squinted in disbelief at this man, old enough to be my dad. 'Sex noises?' I could feel my voice dropping to almost a whisper. 'Like, what noises?'

Kev laughed coldly. 'Come on,' he said. 'You must know what I mean.'

I shrugged and he rolled his eyes. Then, something quite extraordinary happened. Kev threw back his head and started screeching like a hyena, squealing and panting in a weird, high-pitched voice that sounded nothing like his own. I now realise he was imitating a woman having an orgasm, but back then I had absolutely no clue what was going on. He sounded a bit like the blonde woman on Farooq's porn video. It was so funny and ridiculous, as he rolled his eyes back in his head and said things like 'harder' and 'that's good', that I had to hold my school jumper to my face to stifle a laugh.

Suddenly he snapped out of his little performance and shot me a look. 'Finding something funny? I'm trying to help you out here.'

'Sorry,' I mumbled. 'It's just . . .'

But Kev wasn't listening. He was touching me now, on the outside of my knickers and then the inside.

'Lie back,' he told me.

His fingers were cold and rough, and I tensed instinctively as he removed my jumper, undid my school tie, and pushed open the buttons on my blouse.

'Make sex noises,' he coaxed me. I was still trying not to giggle, because I was nervous more than anything. I gave a few weak grunts, but nothing like Kev's screams. 'You can do better than that. Come on.'

I didn't have time to reply, as he was undoing my bra. I looked down to see my bare breasts and I felt the sudden urge to cover them up, but I stayed deathly still, scared of doing the wrong thing and losing my chance to make an easy £17,000.

'Hmm,' he said, as he took them in his cold hands. 'Hmm. Yes, they're quite nice.'

Then, he undid his trousers. Without another word, he climbed on top of me. In that moment, my innocence was gone forever.

6

Innocence Lost

Kev had sex with me for the first and last time that evening. As he entered me, I'd braced myself for it to be really sore, as I'd read in magazines that your first time can be agony. But it wasn't. He was quite small down there and he did it really slowly, so it wasn't so bad. He didn't bother to look for a condom, and I didn't ask why. I just didn't feel like it was my place to say anything and I assumed he knew what he was doing.

Throughout the whole thing he kept telling me to make noises and he'd sometimes break into his ridiculous impression of a woman having sex.

It seemed so alien to me, the concept that a woman could enjoy this so much she'd make such a bloody racket. Sure, I'd expected it to be much worse than it was, but I was still nowhere near making any of Kev's noises without forcing myself.

I kept expecting him to get excited, like Imran had when I'd given him a blow job, or Farooq had been while watching his video. But if Kev was enjoying this, he didn't let on. The only noises he made were those he expected me to imitate and then, abruptly, he stopped. I wondered if he might start again but he climbed off me and told me to get dressed, before hopping back into the front seat and driving off. He hadn't even finished, if you catch my drift, but he didn't seem bothered.

'OK,' he said, starting the car again. 'That wasn't bad. But you need to watch more movies.'

'Movies?' I echoed.

'Yes, movies,' he repeated. 'But not just any movies. Movies like the one you saw Farooq watching. Sex movies.'

I cringed as the image of the blonde woman and her huge breasts flashed back into my mind. 'Right.'

'Remember,' he went on. 'If you want to be good at this, and make good money, you have to be an actress. It's a bit like being in a soap opera. Just think like you're in *EastEnders* – you have to pretend. Watch their faces, watch what they're doing.' He turned to look at me. 'No one will want to pay for you if they don't think you're having a good time.'

As we drove back along the road, the M54 stretching out ahead of us, I felt a little numb. That was it, my first time, with Imran's dad. Even back then I think I knew he'd never had any sexual interest in me. I was just a way for him to make money, quick, easy money. I was a product to him and the pound signs were flashing in his eyes. While Mr Khan continually groped me and stuck his tongue down my throat, Kev was different.

As he indicated to leave the motorway, a few junctions up from Telford, I surveyed his face from the corner of my eye.

I just knew that he'd never touch me again.

'Where are we going?' I asked. I knew he wasn't taking me home, but I didn't feel scared, just curious.

'I just need to pop to this house for half an hour,' he said. 'You can come. I won't be long.'

He left the motorway a few towns up from Telford, in a place I didn't really recognise. He drew up outside a small terraced house with red-brick walls. As he pulled on the handbrake and unclipped his belt, I stayed in my seat.

'Well,' he said. 'Are you coming in or what?'

I thought he was doing another shady business deal, so I was surprised he wanted me to come with him, but I followed dutifully behind. For a moment, I wondered if he was taking me to my first customer, but he swung open the door without knocking. Strewn across the floor in the hallway were various baby toys.

'Daddy!' came a little voice. All of a sudden, a little boy came tearing through the hallway like a mini tornado. He was mixed race, like Imran and Farooq and their sisters, and he had a mop of black hair and a cheeky grin. He couldn't have been more than two years old.

Behind him, in the doorway to the kitchen, was a young woman. She was really glamorous. The first thing I noticed was her shoes: massive brown strappy wedges, probably four or five inches high. Despite this, she was really petite. She wore a fitted denim skirt to her knees, which clung to her perfect figure and showed off her little bum. Her red blouse revealed a hint of cleavage. Her hair was blonde and in very big, loose curls, like she'd spent hours styling it. Her lips were pink and her eyes black with kohl and mascara. As soon as she saw me, she gave me a warm smile.

'Oh, hello, love,' she said. 'And what's this one called, Kev?'

'This is Holly,' Kev said.

The woman smiled again. She was holding a cup of tea in her hand. 'Ah, yes, of course!' she said. 'Your mum works at the school, doesn't she? Come on in. I'm Lisa. Would you like a cup of tea?'

'Er, OK,' I replied. 'Thanks.'

'Not a problem,' Lisa chirped. She didn't flinch as her son tugged at her skirt. 'But you wouldn't mind taking your shoes off, would you, sweetheart? I've just hoovered my carpets. What do you take?'

'Just milk, thanks,' I said, as I took off my black school shoes and left them by the door. Kev did the same.

'Daddy, daddy, daddy,' the little boy said. 'Daddy!'

'Ssh, Saif,' Lisa said. 'Honestly, he's been playing up *all day*. Won't go to bed until his dad gets in. It drives me bloody daft, so it does.'

Saif bounded into Kev's arms and he picked him up.

'Go on into the lounge,' Lisa told me. She was standing next to me now, and I was close enough to smell her expensive perfume. She was towering over me in her wedges but I didn't dare ask why only she was allowed to wear shoes in the house.

'Make yourself at home while I put the kettle on. Kev, could you try and get him down? He's been running riot all day. Honestly, Holly, I don't know how I manage sometimes.'

As I was left alone with Lisa, and the kettle whistled in the background, I felt really weird. It was strange to know that Kev had yet another girlfriend and family, but that wasn't what surprised me the most. Lisa was so glamorous. She looked a bit like a Barbie doll. She obviously took care of herself, and her house was immaculate.

She was the kind of woman who'd probably be able to go out on a Saturday night and pull pretty much any guy she wanted. What the hell was she doing with a scruffy middle-aged man like Kev? I wondered if she knew she was sharing him with two others. Surely she must have an idea. Why else didn't Kev live with her, or offer to marry her? Why else was she left looking after little Saif on her own?

'Here you go, darling,' she said sweetly, as she handed me my tea and plonked herself next to me on the sofa. 'Milk, no sugar.'

'Thanks,' I replied. Suddenly I was struck by the most awful pang of guilt. What if she didn't know about Liz and Kev's Pakistani wife? What if he'd spun her some crazy story and she thought she was the only woman in his life? Then I thought about what we'd just done and I felt a little knot form in my stomach – a horrible, gnawing knot of guilt.

This woman has just made me a cup of tea, I thought. I'm sitting on her couch, drinking from her mug, she's calling me sweetheart and love and darling, and I've just had sex with her boyfriend. What kind of person does that make me?

Maybe it shows how well Kev and the others had groomed me that I'd already started to blame myself for the situation. Instead of wondering why Lisa didn't bat an eyelid at having a random fourteen-year-old in her front room, brought there by her scruffy lover, I blamed myself for being there. Here she was, being so nice to me, and I'd just shagged the father of her child in the back of his car.

God, I told myself. You really are a bloody slag, aren't you?

Lisa swept her mass of blonde hair over her shoulder, as she reached into an expensive-looking handbag, from which she produced an even more expensive-looking mobile phone. 'Excuse me a sec,' she said. 'Just sending a quick text.'

I scanned her front room as she tapped away on her phone with her perfectly manicured nails, the same shade of pink as her lips. The room was full of nice things: an expensive leather sofa, dozens of pricey-looking toys for Saif and a big flat-screen TV.

'Your house is lovely,' I said, without quite meaning to.

Lisa's face lit up. 'Oh, thanks, love,' she said. 'D'you like it? I've been doing it up bit by bit. I've just done the kitchen. I want to do the garden next. I'd really like a lovely rose bush. I keep on at Kev to buy me one but he says he buys me enough things!' She tipped back her head and her blonde hair fell around her shoulders, as she let out a girly laugh. 'Men, eh? What are they *like*? They just don't understand these things.'

I stayed silent.

'Anyway,' she went on. 'I'll have plenty of time on my hands when Saif starts going to nursery a few days a week. Don't know what I'll do with myself, to be honest! But I do like the idea of being a lady of leisure. Doesn't that sound fun?'

I had no idea. 'I guess,' I shrugged. I didn't ask if she had a job, or planned to get one. I think I already had my answer. Saif was the same age as Amy, but Mum was run ragged trying to make ends meet as she juggled work and her kids. Although Saif was a real livewire, Lisa's life was very different.

Kev appeared in the doorway. 'That's him off,' he said. 'Finally.'

Lisa rolled her eyes. 'Thank God.' She turned to me, and gave me a friendly nudge. 'Kev comes in and does all the nice, fun things and Saif thinks he's the best thing since sliced bread. Won't go to bed without his daddy. Of course, he doesn't listen to a bloody word I say all day.'

I studied Kev's face for a flicker of a reaction, but there was none.

'Anyway,' Lisa said, breezily. 'Shouldn't you be getting Holly home?'

'Relax,' Kev said. 'You're fine, aren't you? It's not that late.'

I opened my mouth to reply, but I wasn't sure what answer was expected of me.

Lisa's beaming smile slipped for just a second. In almost a whisper, she said: 'Come on, Kev. We don't want her mum wondering where she's got to, do we?'

After he'd tested me out, Kev wasted no time in getting me to work. My first customer was on a Tuesday night – I remember it really clearly. I'd been dropped at the roadside by Mr Khan as usual when my phone started buzzing with a call from my new boss, so to speak.

'Be ready at half past five,' Kev said. 'I'll pick you up at the end of your road. And don't be late.'

Mum was taking Lauren and Amy somewhere after work – I can't remember where. She'd told me she'd sort our dinner when she was back around seven, but I sent her a text and told her Carly had invited me round to hers instead, and not to bother with my tea. A perfectly reasonable explanation. Why would she ask any questions?

I wasn't sure how long Kev would keep me out. How long did these things take? I didn't have a clue. I knew I'd be really hungry now I'd told Mum not to keep me any food, so I took one of those horrible ready-made bags of mashed potato and shoved it in the microwave. When it was ready, I squeezed in loads of tomato ketchup to give it some flavour. It was nothing like a proper dinner, and a bit lumpy, but it didn't taste as minging as I'd expected, and at least it would fill me up.

Then I went upstairs and took off my school uniform, carefully selecting a pair of loose-fitting leggings and a denim jacket. I'd guessed Kev wasn't exactly going to take me to meet anyone who was young and fit, but I thought I might as well try to make myself look presentable, to boost my chances of getting good money.

After all, that's what this was about. Money. Kev was going to make me some really, really good money.

A couple of minutes later, my phone began buzzing again.

'I'm at the end of your road,' Kev said. 'Now, be quick. This man's wife is only out for a couple of hours. We can't waste any time.'

I put my phone in my pocket and ran out to the end of the road, where he was sitting waiting in his car, drumming his fingers against the steering wheel. For a moment, it felt like he was my dad and he was driving me to school or something, getting impatient as he waited. As soon as I climbed into the passenger seat, he let off the handbrake and went tearing down the road.

'This man is rich,' Kev explained, as the streets flashed by. 'He owns a big shop in town. Every Tuesday, his wife goes out to visit her sister.' We pulled up at some traffic lights and he took his eyes off the road for a second to look me square in the eye. 'But she's always, always back sharp at half-seven. So we have to make sure we get there in time for you to go in, do your bit, and get back out before she comes home. You get me?'

I looked at the clock on the dashboard, which told me it was a quarter to six. 'Right,' I said. 'How long will it take?'

Kev let out a weak sigh. 'It takes however long it takes, Holly. Just make sure you're done before the wife gets back or there will be big trouble for all of us. Don't mess about, is what I'm saying.'

We drove in silence for a few more minutes before Kev pulled up outside a really fancy house. It was detached, with a massive, well-kept garden. From the outside, it looked like it had five, maybe six, bedrooms.

I expected Kev to bundle me straight into the house, desperate to get me in and out as soon as he could, so I was surprised when he parked up and turned the ignition off, stopping me just as I moved to open the door on the passenger side.

'Don't go in just yet, hold on a minute. There's a few things we need to get straight first.'

I took my hand away from the door handle. 'Like what?'

'Well, if he asks,' Kev said, 'your name isn't Holly. You're Nikki, and you're fifteen. Got it?'

I nodded. I didn't see what difference it made, whether I was fourteen or fifteen, but I wasn't about to argue with Kev. Despite what he was doing, I still looked up to him a bit because he was a dad and he had kids my age.

'And don't let him think you're stupid,' he added. 'He's not to take you for a mug, the dirty old bastard. Sex is £200. And if he tries to do it without a condom, it's a £25 charge. Make sure he knows that. OK?'

'OK,' I echoed.

'Right, on you go, then,' he said. 'He's left the door open for you.'

Maybe I should have been nervous as I walked up the long garden path and took the big stone steps, one by one. But I didn't feel anything, really. I just wanted to get it over with and get my share of the money. I'd already blocked out what I was going to do and what it meant. Anyway, even if I wanted to back out now, I couldn't. Kev would go mad.

The main front door was ajar, just like Kev had said it would be. The house was as grand inside as it was outside. The smell of expensive furniture polish wafted through my nostrils, as I instinctively wiped my feet on the mat and gazed along the long, sweeping hallway, with its large oriental ornaments and freshly arranged flowers. At the other end of the corridor, the door to the lounge lay open. I could see that it was full of expensive, luxurious furniture. I just stood there for a second, before a little Chinese man popped out from another of the rooms.

He was about sixty, and really, really small. By that point I'd grown to around five foot seven and I towered over him. He was peering over thick varifocal glasses. We stood staring wordlessly at each other for a few seconds.

I expected him to say hello, maybe to ask how I was or even for my name. I silently reminded myself that I was Nikki, not Holly, and I was fifteen, not fourteen. It almost made it all a little bit easier, pretending to be someone else. Maybe Kev was right. Maybe it was all about being an actress after all.

But the first thing the man said to me was: 'Go upstairs. First bedroom on the left. And take your clothes off.'

His accent was strong, but his English seemed good. I didn't say a word, as I obediently walked up the stairs. I pushed open the first door on the left to find a big, king-sized bed. The room was large, with an expensive wooden dressing table and a big mirror. I made a mental note not to look in its direction, as I didn't really want to see what I was doing.

I took off my leggings, then my top. I was standing in my underwear when the man pushed open the door. He didn't say anything, as he too began removing his clothes. I instinctively shielded my eyes, as the thought of seeing him undress embarrassed me, despite what I was there to do. When I turned around again, he was standing in just his little white pants. He had tufts of dark hair all over his short, scrawny body.

'No condom,' he said. 'Two hundred and twenty.'

I remembered what Kev had said about not letting him take me for a mug and I shook my head. 'No.'

'No?' he repeated.

'No, it's two hundred and twenty *with* a condom,' I said. 'You have to pay more if you want to do it without one.'

Perhaps I should have been thinking about my health. If this man paid for sex, he could have had all sorts of nasty diseases that could be passed on to me. And then, of course, there was the possibility I could get pregnant. But all I was thinking of was Kev and how I was scared he'd be mad if I came back short on the money. Maybe he'd just drop me and I'd never have the chance to make my £17,000. After all, he'd had sex with me without a condom and I'd just put it to the back of my mind.

But he hadn't finished, so there was no risk of pregnancy, or so I told myself.

The man shrugged and gestured to me to lie down on the bed. I did as he said. He sidled up beside me and said, 'Suck me.'

I looked at him and I almost laughed. He was so little and pathetic and he couldn't have scared me if he'd tried. He was nothing like Mr Khan or Kev or even the teenage boys who shouted abuse at me in the street.

'No,' I said firmly. 'That's not what I'm here for. I'm here for sex.'

I even surprised myself at how confident I sounded. My voice didn't even waver. I glanced down at his crotch and he was already hard. He paused for a few minutes but he didn't argue with what I'd said. He simply took a condom from its wrapper and fiddled with it as he tried to put it on. He said something in his own language – something that sounded like a swear word – as he struggled to get it on. He seemed agitated, on edge. I looked at a clock on the wall, which told me it was now a quarter past six. We still had over an hour until his wife was home, but I figured maybe he was scared she'd come home early and find him in bed with a teenage girl.

Eventually he managed to get the condom on. As he rolled on top of me, pulling my pants down and awkwardly unhooking my bra, I couldn't help but wonder if this was the bed he shared with his wife. The room was immaculate, but there were no personal touches, no signs of life. No make-up on the dressing table, or clothes draped over a chair. I figured that we were probably in the spare room. I couldn't imagine he'd want to risk having the smell of another woman – or girl, in this case – on their sheets. I wondered what kind of marriage they had. Did they talk, or kiss, or even have sex themselves? Or did they live separate lives under the same roof, unhappy together but scared to part?

As he entered me, my train of thought was interrupted. He was really small down there, so I could hardly feel him, as he gave a couple of weak thrusts, and some hollow little grunts.

But before I had time to look around the room, it was over. He let out a barely audible moan and that was it. Done. He climbed off me and took off the condom.

'Go into the bathroom and clean yourself up,' he ordered. He didn't meet my eye.

I felt a bit strange – the sex had been so brief I wasn't really in too much of a mess, if truth be told, but I grabbed my clothes and went into the en-suite bathroom, where I hastily pulled them on again. I looked at myself in the mirror, just the same as before. Nothing has changed, I told myself. I'm just making a bit of extra cash. What's so bad about that?

When I came out, the man had got dressed too. He'd put his glasses back on and he was counting out a wad of twenty-pound notes. He looked up and pressed them into my hand.

'Two hundred and twenty,' he said. 'I will see you next week.'

7

Into the Trap

I got in the car and handed the notes straight to Kev. I'd already hurriedly counted them out as I walked down the garden path, making sure the full two hundred and twenty was there and the client hadn't taken me for a mug, like Kev had warned me he might.

Kev started to count them, too, and he stopped in his tracks as he got to the end of the pile.

'There's only two hundred and twenty here,' he said. His brown, leathery face was contorted with anger. 'You're a fiver short.'

I couldn't understand why he was getting so worked up over a fiver but I didn't have time to reply. He thrust the notes in my face and said: 'I told you not to let him do it without a condom unless he paid two hundred and twenty-five!'

It was the first time Kev had raised his voice to me — like, properly shouted. I guess I'd always been a bit scared of him, even though he didn't seem as aggressive as Mr Khan. There was just something about him that said: don't mess, or there'll be trouble.

'He used a condom,' I said. Proudly, I added, 'It's just that I managed to get an extra twenty quid off him.'

Kev started the engine, but his eyes weren't on the road. He was looking from me to the money to me again, as if he wasn't sure he believed me.

'Right,' he said. 'Well you better be telling the bloody truth. Because if you haven't used a condom, you'll need to use some of your own money to get the morning-after pill. And it's up to you to get it, by the way.'

I hadn't thought about getting the morning-after pill. I'd heard of it, of course, and I knew it stopped you getting pregnant, but I didn't know where to buy it or how it actually worked.

'Well, he used one,' I said. 'So it's fine. And he told me he'd see me next week.'

Kev's expression suddenly changed and his black eyes lit up. 'Did he? That's good. You must have done all right then.'

He sounded almost proud, like I was his daughter and I'd told him I'd come top of the class in a test.

I shrugged. 'It didn't last very long,' I said, honestly.

Kev let out a little chuckle. 'Ha!' he said. 'Sad little fucker. Sad, sad little fucker.'

I quickly came to realise that he talked about all of his so-called clients like this. He had almost as little respect for them as he did for the girls he sold to them without a second thought, but he knew his market. Most of them were sex-deprived and lonely: immigrants who knew no one in the UK and couldn't meet women because of the language barrier, and older men trapped in loveless marriages and communities which frowned upon divorce. Of course, there were also those who were too downright minging and filthy to ever attract a woman in the normal way – but I'd get to know all about them later.

'Can you drop me at the phone box?' I asked, as we drew back into my part of town. Kev stopped the car and handed me three, crisp, twenty-pound notes.

'Here you go,' he said. 'Sixty quid.'

I shut the car door and called Carly straight away.

'Come and meet me by the phone box,' I told her. 'Imran's dad just gave me sixty quid.'

'Sixty quid!' she echoed. 'Amazing! I'll be ten minutes.'

It was certainly true that sixty quid was a fortune to us. Although neither of us had ever gone without, we didn't come from wealthy families and we most definitely had never been given this much money in one go before. What stunned me the most was how easy it had all been. I'd barely had to do anything. The little Chinese man must have been inside me for a minute, two maximum. I could barely feel anything, and yet I'd come away with sixty quid. Sixty bloody quid!

I thought: Kev was right. It really is easy money.

I was so excited it took me a few minutes to do the maths, to work out that the Chinese man had paid Kev two hundred and twenty quid, so he'd given me sixty and kept one hundred and sixty. It was hardly a fair split, considering I'd done all of the work. But I shrugged it all off. I figured that Kev would start giving me more money the more experienced I got. He'd just given me sixty this time because he wasn't sure that I'd really known what I was doing. Lily Brown had probably been doing it for ages, so maybe her cut had gone up every time. Maybe that's how she got the £17,000.

Carly came bounding down the street a few minutes later, her ponytail flapping in the wind and her fat spilling out of the jeans I'd noticed were now a size too small.

'Sixty quid!' she shouted, while she was still yards from me. 'How the hell?'

'Sssh!' I said to her. 'You don't want someone to hear.'

'Well, what did you have to do?' she asked. 'You must have done something to get sixty quid.' Suddenly realisation shot across her face. 'Oh shit! You did what Lily Brown's been doing, didn't you? Did you shag someone for money?'

Her words made me flinch a little but I kept my cool. 'Don't say it like that,' I said. 'It's not as bad as it sounds. It's the easiest sixty quid you'll ever make in your life. You just lie there.'

Carly giggled. 'What was it like? Who was it?'

'Oh, just some old guy,' I said. 'It was over, like, straight away, and his dick was tiny. I couldn't even feel it.'

We both laughed.

'It's well easier than a blow job,' I said. 'You don't have to do anything. What should we spend the money on, then? Shall we top up our phones?'

We walked to the nearest corner shop and I bought us each a twenty-quid top-up. Then we bought some sweets and crisps, like we had whenever Mr Khan had given me money, except we had a bit more this time, so we went a bit wild and ended up with too much to carry. By the time we'd finished, I had barely more than a tenner left, but I wasn't really too bothered. After all, I was seeing the same client again the next week and I'd get more money then, wouldn't I?

'I don't think I've ever had a twenty-quid top-up,' Carly said. 'Not in one go. Hey, do you think Imran's dad would let me do what you do? It sounds like a piece of piss.'

'I can ask,' I said. 'See what he says.'

Before it was time to meet the Tuesday night man again, I got another appointment. It was the following Monday, and I was sitting at the end of the dirt track in Mr Khan's car. He was stroking my leg and I was trying to distract myself by focusing on a horse meandering through a field in the distance, at the edge of the horizon. I could feel his horrible hot breath on my cheek, and it turned my stomach. My phone was buzzing furiously in my pocket but I didn't dare answer it because I knew what would happen: Mr Khan would go mental and leave me to walk home. It was another ten minutes before he drove me back to the phone box where I'd arranged to meet Carly and, by that time, I had loads of missed calls and a voicemail from Kev.

'Why the hell haven't you been answering?' he thundered down the line, when I eventually called back. 'I need you to go somewhere tonight.'

I didn't know what to say. I didn't want to say I'd been with Mr Khan, partly because I was ashamed and partly because I knew that would make Kev even madder – that I'd gone off with an older man and he wasn't making any money out of it.

'Can you be at the phone box in five minutes?' he asked. 'Answer me!'

'Yes, yes,' I said. 'Oh, but can my friend maybe come? She wants to do it too.'

For someone who seemed to be in such a hurry, Kev paused

for a long time at the end of the line. 'Maybe,' he said. 'It depends. Just bring her anyway.'

Thankfully Carly appeared before Kev did and when his car came tearing down the street, we both climbed in: Carly in the back, and me in the passenger seat next to Kev. He looked round at Carly, giving her a good stare, taking in all of her features and her figure.

Then he turned back round and started the car again. 'Oh yeah,' he said to me, as if she wasn't there. His voice was a bit flat. 'I've seen her with you before.'

Kev drove through the town for five or ten minutes before he turned the car into his own street, the one I'd visited with him several times before. At first, I got a sinking feeling in my stomach. I didn't want him to take me into his house to meet a man, to make me walk past Farooq and Imran, and watch them smirk as some stranger led me up to the bedroom.

Just think of the money, I told myself. It's money. It's just a job. A very, very easy job. They already think you're a slag. What difference does this make?

But Kev said, 'We're not going to my house. We're using the one next door.'

'What?' I said. 'Why? How can you do that?'

'Because I just can,' he said. 'It's mine, too.'

'Oh,' I said. 'Who's there, then?'

'Just another sad old bastard,' he replied. 'Make it quick this time. I need to get over to Lisa's before Saif goes to bed or she'll go mad.'

Even then, it made me feel a little strange that Kev could talk so casually about putting his son to bed as he was about to send me, an underage girl, into a house to pleasure a stranger for money. I tried not to think about his own daughters, just a few years younger than I was, caring for their mother just yards away, or to contemplate what he would have done if they'd done something like this.

'Should I go in, too?' Carly asked, eagerly. 'Is there just one? If there's a couple maybe I can help out. I'm good at giving blow jobs.'

I cringed inwardly, wishing for a moment that I'd never invited her along, as Kev muttered under his breath, 'I'm sure you are, sweetheart.'

'What was that?' Carly asked. 'Do you want me to go too? Will I get sixty quid if I go?'

Kev turned round and smirked at my friend. 'Just leave it to Holly. You stay in the back.'

Now, it makes me feel a bit sick to think of how brainwashed Carly was, how brainwashed we both were. It chills me to the bone, as an adult, to think how eager we both were to sell our bodies to the highest bidder, at just fourteen years old, for some phone credit and a packet of crisps. But back then I felt a bit embarrassed for Carly.

I knew as soon as Kev had first cast his eye over her that she wasn't what he was looking for. We were simply products to him, and he clearly didn't place much value on her because she was so overweight. Now that we could buy all the crisps and sweets and fizzy drinks we wanted, she was only getting bigger. Kev knew more men would pay for me, because I was thinner. It sounds really mean, but even then I'd sussed what was going on.

I didn't want to hang around and look at Carly's confused, crushed face, so I followed Kev out of the car and into the terraced house. A woman walking her dog did a double take as she saw Kev and me file through the door. I didn't recognise her, but my stomach instantly twisted as that awful thought shot to the surface of my mind.

What if she knows my mum?

I didn't have much time to dwell on it, though, as Kev pushed open the front door and led me into the lounge. It was like a mirror image of the one in the house next door, with some nice furniture and a flat-screen TV, the kind of room that wouldn't look odd if you walked past and just happened to glance in. The only thing missing was the school pictures, but I felt glad Imran and Farooq weren't grinning down from the walls.

My eyes travelled to the sofa, where my next customer was sitting.

If I'd thought the first man was old, this guy was positively decrepit. He must have been at least in his seventies, perhaps even older. He was Chinese, too, and even smaller than the first client. He stood up to get a proper look at me and he barely reached to my shoulder. He was wearing a suit, as if it was some sort of special occasion, and that almost made me laugh. It was ridiculous. He looked like he was about to splash out on a meal in a fancy restaurant, rather than pay for a fourteen-year-old girl. His skin was discoloured and patchy, and his white hair was really thin, and combed over the top of his head.

'He doesn't speak English,' Kev said. 'Take him to the back room.'

If the front room in Kev's other house looked like people could have lived there, the rest of it was a very different story. I quickly realised that this house existed solely for this purpose, somewhere for dirty old men to do dirty deeds away from the prying eyes of the outside world.

You had to hand it to Kev. He really had thought of his customers' every need. I caught sight of what I guessed should have been the kitchen, but there was no cooker or washing machine or microwave, just piles and piles of junk and a bad, mouldy smell. The back room was even worse. You could hardly move for boxes and there was a rotten, moth-eaten sofa bed and a halogen heater in the corner of the room. The damp was so putrid it almost knocked me sideways, but the old man didn't seem bothered at all.

I couldn't help wondering where he lived, and if he had a wife at home and what she'd make of all this if she found out. I tried to dismiss the pang of guilt I felt when I thought of him having a home and a family. It did make me feel like a slag, shagging other women's husbands for money, but I tried not to dwell on it. I just hoped we wouldn't get caught out because then it would all be my fault.

It would all be my fault, for being such a slag.

The man gestured to my boobs and I guessed he wanted me to take my clothes off. Robotically I undressed, and then sat on the sofa beside him. He was down to his pants now and his wrinkly, saggy skin made me feel a bit sick.

He said something in his own language, which sounded a bit like a question.

'Eh?' I said.

But he just shook his head. I figured he wanted me to lie back, so that's what I did. I looked at the ceiling and watched, as a fly buzzed around the naked lightbulb.

I waited for him to do the inevitable, as he cupped my bare breasts and gave a weak moan. It took me a few seconds to realise it was over.

We hadn't even started having sex and that was him, done.

I sat bolt upright and pulled my T-shirt over my head, feeling smug. This just gets easier every time, I thought. I wondered how much he'd paid. Had he intended to use a condom or not? Still, I figured he'd paid at least two hundred quid. Two hundred quid, to touch a girl's boobs for two seconds! Kev was right. These guys really were pretty bloody sad. I almost felt sorry for them.

As I was getting dressed, I could hear my phone vibrating in my pocket. I looked at the number on the screen and saw it was Beaver, as I'd christened him – the guy who'd showed me his dick at the foot of the Wrekin. He called me sometimes, but nowhere near as often as Kev and Mr Khan. He'd got my number from somewhere after that night, but he seemed harmless enough, so I didn't really mind. Plus, half the Asian men in Telford had my number anyway. What odds did another one make?

I thought about answering but the old man was watching me as I pulled my T-shirt over my head, phone still in hand. I quickly cancelled the call.

The old man was standing, counting out a pile of ten- and twenty-pound notes and handing them to Kev, as I walked back into the lounge. Without even looking in my direction, he nodded to Kev and disappeared out of the front door, back into the night.

I stood there, expectantly, waiting for my sixty quid, wondering if I'd maybe get more this time because it was my second customer, as Kev checked and double checked the little man had paid the full amount.

Eventually, he handed me two twenty-pound notes. I looked at him, confused, and he rolled his eyes.

'You could at least look happy,' he said. 'Forty quid for ten minutes' work.'

I slowly met his gaze. 'I thought it was supposed to be sixty. Last time I got sixty.'

Kev lowered his thick, black eyebrows and looked straight at me. 'Don't fucking start, Holly. I know you didn't shag him. Did you?'

I didn't know what to say. 'I . . .'

'Sad old prick like that just touched your boobs and came straight away,' he said. 'Am I right?'

I nodded, slowly.

'Of course I am,' he said. 'So don't you ever try to pull the wool over my eyes again. You take what you're given. This costs me money, you know. I have to heat this place. I have to drive you here. I pay all the bills, I find all the men, I do all the work, yet you've got the cheek to ask for more?'

I shrugged, defiantly, as he threw open the front door and together we walked towards the car, where Carly was still sitting in the back seat. The orange glow from the streetlights shone onto the pavement.

Kev paused before he opened the door and said: 'You should be fucking grateful you even got that much.'

8

Bought and Sold

I was in a bit of a mood when Kev dropped me at the end of the road. I didn't even really want to speak to Carly. I thought he'd maybe relent when he saw I was a bit pissed off that he'd given me twenty quid less than before, but he didn't say a word until he stopped the car.

'Remember,' he said. 'Tuesday night. And don't be late.'

'Right,' I said, before letting Carly out the back and slamming the door with an almighty thud. Kev's car sped off into the distance and I kicked some gravel beneath my feet.

'What's up?' Carly said. 'You seem annoyed. Didn't you just get sixty quid?'

I shrugged. 'Nope. Forty. The guy just touched my boobs, so Kev wouldn't give me any more.'

'It's better than nothing,' she replied. 'Do you think he'll let me do it?'

I didn't want to say anything to hurt her, so I mumbled something about not being sure how many men there were. She seemed oblivious to the fact that I was trying to let her down gently.

'I'd love £17,000,' she said. 'Lily Brown must have shagged

so many guys to get that much. Do you think he gives you more the more times you do it? I bet he does.'

I didn't know what to say. I looked at my watch and it was long past my curfew. I already had a missed call from Mum and I was starving.

'I better go, Carls,' I said. 'See you tomorrow.'

When I walked in, Mum said something to me about home-work but it didn't really register. I just went upstairs and put my headphones on. I'd become obsessed with the rapper Ja Rule, a far cry from the innocent chart music I'd once danced to awkwardly in the snooker hall. Some of his songs were a bit explicit, but they suited my mood. More often than not I was in a bit of a huff and tonight was no different.

As I walked home from school the next night, my phone started to buzz with a call from Mr Khan. I was feeling a little more defiant than usual, maybe because I was still wound up about Kev selling me short. I cancelled the call and continued to walk down the hill, hoping against hope that he wouldn't drive past.

It was only a matter of seconds before I could feel my phone vibrating in my pocket again. I didn't dare take it out. I picked up the pace and practically ran all the way home. I just wasn't in the mood for Mr Khan and his wandering hands. I couldn't face him that day.

I felt a momentary sense of relief as I stepped over the threshold and into Mum's front room, but I might have known that there would be consequences. There always were with Mr Khan. It was just like the day I'd gone to Jenny's and he'd been so mad.

For the next fifteen minutes he called me constantly. As soon as I cancelled one call, he'd ring again. It was like he had me on redial. I could feel the anger and frustration bubbling up inside me and for a second I thought about smashing my phone against the living-room wall.

Eventually I decided I'd be better off just answering it. Mum was due home from work any second and, even though it was on silent, I didn't want her to see me cancelling the calls or to hear it vibrating in my pocket.

Mr Khan was fuming. 'Why don't you answer?' he screamed. 'Why, Holly? Why?'

I stayed silent, as he ranted and raved in his broken English for a few minutes. I couldn't understand most of what he was saying, but I knew it wasn't pleasant. Eventually he calmed down and his voice dropped a little: 'You meet me tomorrow,' he said. 'Or I tell your mum you are prostitute.'

As he rang off, I could feel the blood pumping through my veins and rushing to my head. A huge knot formed in my stomach and I felt physically sick. It was my worst fear – Mum finding out what I was up to. Mr Khan never missed an opportunity to remind me that his daughter went to the school where Mum worked, and I was absolutely terrified he'd say something. I didn't know if he knew about Kev, but the Asian community in Telford was small, so it was definitely possible.

Needless to say, the next day I made sure I answered when Mr Khan called. I waited for him exactly where he'd told me to and I didn't protest as he bundled me into the car. He didn't have to tell me to lie flat in the back. I did it without being asked.

When the car slowed to a halt, I realised we were at the end of the dirt track, as usual. I couldn't help but think how idyllic it all looked: the horses running playfully in the field in the distance and the acres of lush woodland all around. It seemed so surreal that I was here with a strange older man who was threatening to tell my mum I was a prostitute.

He ordered me to get into the front. I managed to stifle a sigh as I prepared for him to touch my legs and shove his horrible tongue down my throat. But he didn't move.

For a few moments he just sat there staring at me with those evil black eyes that still make me shudder. I didn't know where to look, so I stared straight ahead, focusing on the horses rather than the uncomfortable situation I was in. For a moment, I ached to run out of the car and towards the field, and to keep running until Mr Khan was far out of sight. But he'd only find me again and I couldn't live with the consequences of disobeying him. He'd sounded so serious when he threatened to tell Mum I was a prostitute and I didn't want to take any chances.

It seemed like an eternity before he broke the silence.

'Holly,' he said. 'You answer phone when I call. OK?'

I nodded. 'OK, OK,' I said. 'I'll answer the phone.'

Mr Khan was still looking at me, his eyes boring into me. Then, he said something that made me almost retch in sheer disgust.

His brown eyes widened as he declared, 'I'm going to fuck you, Holly.'

My whole body tensed in horror. Kissing Mr Khan was bad enough but the thought of him lying on top of me was just too much to bear. I could feel the bile rising in my throat and the panic spreading across my face. I opened my mouth to say no, I didn't want to, but no words came out. I tried to protest again, but I clamped my mouth shut as it dawned on me that there was no point in resisting. If I didn't do exactly as he said, he'd go straight to Mum and say the unthinkable and then my life would be ruined.

'I'm going to fuck you,' he said again. It was almost like he was testing me, trying to coax me into responding. I stayed silent. 'I'm going to fuck you. Get in the back.'

Wordlessly I did as he said. Suddenly I was beyond tears. When I think of it now, I'm amazed at how quickly I managed to resign myself to my fate. I had no option but to have this horrible man lie on top of me and violate me in the most horrific way. The best I could hope for was that it would be quick.

As he pulled down his grubby white trousers, the smell of him was almost too much. He'd clearly never heard of deodorant and he absolutely stunk of sweat. I'm not sure if he smelled worse that day than any other, but it certainly seemed like it. His stench filled the whole car.

'Do you want me to fuck you or make sex with you?' he barked.

I just lay there, mouth half-open, not quite knowing what to say. I didn't understand the difference between 'fucking' and 'making sex', and I wasn't sure what the right answer was. I wondered if something had got lost in translation but I was scared to say anything in case it made Mr Khan even angrier than he already seemed.

'I don't care,' I said, eventually. 'Just do it.'

He started to paw at the leggings I'd hastily pulled on before he'd asked me to meet him and soon they were round my ankles. Next came my pants. He tugged at my hair so violently I almost cried out and I had to bite down on my lip so I didn't make any noise, as he threw me on the back seat and climbed on top of me.

It won't be that bad, I told myself. It won't be that bad. Think of Kev, and the Chinese man. It didn't hurt, it was over in no time. This will be just the same.

But as much as I tried to persuade myself it would be bearable, I knew in my heart of hearts it would be awful. I held my breath and Mr Khan forced himself on top of me and inside me. His awful, sweaty smell filled my nostrils. The pain was instant. He was much bigger than Kev or the Chinese man and it really, really hurt, but I knew if I made a sound in protest he'd go mad and who knew what would happen then?

He wasn't a big man, but his weight on top of me felt suffocating and I could barely breathe as he started to thrust in and out of me. I winced in pain with every move he made. He was so forceful, so violent, that my head kept hitting the car door.

I decided to look at the horses in the distance, watching them jump around and frolic in the grass, in a desperate bid to block out what was going on.

Mr Khan lasted a lot longer than the Chinese man but, thankfully, it was still over within about ten minutes. When he'd finished, he practically pushed me out of the way as he scrambled to put his trousers back on.

Then, without a hint of emotion, he said: 'I like you.'

I just stared at the horizon, still watching the horses, as I pulled my leggings up.

'Holly!' he said. His voice was laced with venom and rage, as he grabbed my arm and pulled my body towards his once more. I held my breath so I didn't have to smell him again. 'I like you. Do you like me?'

Just for a moment, the fear inside me evaporated and I shook my head. 'No,' I replied, honestly.

Of course, this was a massive mistake.

'I'll slap you!' he screeched. 'You fucking bitch! Do you like me?'

I closed my eyes, just for a fraction of a second, hoping that when I opened them I'd be somewhere, anywhere that wasn't the inside of Mr Khan's Nissan.

But there was no escape. I was here and I'd have to keep coming here whenever he wanted or risk him telling Mum everything. There was only one answer I was allowed to give: 'Yes. I like you.'

It was like he hadn't heard me.

'You do as I say,' he said. 'Or I rape your mum. I come for your sisters and I rape your mum.'

As I lay down in the back of the car on the journey home along the dirt track, my pain hidden from the world, I wanted so badly to cry but no tears would come. With tears came a sort of release, even if it was only temporary. Instead I felt on edge, with a gnawing, horrible knot in the pit of my stomach. It was one thing threatening to tell Mum I was a prostitute. It was another threatening to rape her, to put her through the awful ordeal I'd just been through myself. How could I ever, ever live with myself if I allowed that to happen?

Nausea swept over me as I pondered on what he'd said about my sisters. How did he even know I had sisters? It was pointless trying to figure it all out, because he knew everything about me there possibly was to know, and he'd use it all against me. I could barely get enough air into my lungs as I thought of poor little Lauren and Amy, so young and innocent, so unaware of the evils that existed in the world as they squabbled over their dolls and watched *The Powerpuff Girls*. What did he mean when he said he'd come for them? Would he rape them too?

I felt so, so guilty. I'd taken this man's money, I'd let him buy me food, and I'd fallen straight into his trap. It was my own fault for being so stupid, for ever answering the phone to him and giving him the time of day.

Now, I had two choices: obey his every command and have him use and abuse me, like a piece of meat. Put up with the constant phone calls, the rough, painful sex and the abuse. Or, risk saying something and have him do to Mum – and maybe, God forbid, my little sisters – what he'd done to me.

What else could I do, but never defy this man again?

It was only when Mr Khan dumped me by the phone box that I remembered it was a Tuesday. I was already late for Kev and the Chinese man.

Kev screeched up beside me and threw open the passenger door without even pulling on his handbrake. I don't know if he'd seen me getting out of Mr Khan's car but, if he had, he didn't say.

'Late again,' he spat. 'You better not fuck this up, Holly. He's one of my best customers.'

I sighed. 'I won't.'

'Yeah, well, we can't piss him off,' Kev went on. 'OK?'

Luckily the Chinese man was as quick as ever. It sounds silly, but compared to Mr Khan it was a walk in the park. He was much smaller and much less rough and I could just lie there and block out what was happening. It was over in no time.

I got back into the car and handed Kev the money, which he counted as meticulously as usual. Thankfully he gave me sixty quid, just like the first time. I folded it carefully and put it in my purse. He drove me to the end of the street, like nothing had happened.

'Tomorrow, I have someone new for you,' he said. 'I'll call you.'

I nodded and closed the car door, before walking to my front gate. I was in a bit of a trance, like I was some sort of zombie. In the space of just a few hours I'd slept with two different men, both old enough to be my dad. Six months ago, I'd have been horrified and repulsed if someone my age had told me they'd done that.

Now, I just felt empty.

'Have you been at Carly's?' Mum called, as I walked through the door. 'Would you like some dinner?'

I nodded, as Amy toddled along and jumped into my arms. I'd always loved playing with her but, as I picked her up for a cuddle, I couldn't stop thinking about what Mr Khan had said. As I held her close to me she chattered away, but my brain couldn't process a word she said. She was just two years old. How could I let anyone hurt her, ever? I had to do everything in my power to stop it.

Suddenly I thought of my purse and the sixty quid. My stomach lurched again, as I wondered what Mum would do if she were to go through it and find all the money. How would I ever explain the fact I had so much cash on me? She'd probably think I'd nicked it and go mental.

I put Amy down and quickly dashed upstairs to the room I shared with Gemma. Our house was so crowded that Gemma now spent lots of her time at Dad's, so I often had the room to myself. Now, I was happier than ever at that prospect. One of the wooden floorboards was a little loose, so I pulled it up and shoved the wad of ten- and twenty-pound notes underneath it before going back downstairs for dinner.

The next evening, Mr Khan picked me up again. This time, he took me to the car park at the foot of the Wrekin. I lay motionless in the back as he had rough, angry sex with me. He chucked me a tenner when he dropped me back on the main road, but I'd quickly got past caring. A tenner was nothing compared to what Kev gave me, yet the sex was ten times worse with Mr Khan than it was with the Chinese man.

I quickly ran home, threw the money under the floorboard with the other notes, and told Mum I was off to meet Carly. My phone was already ringing with a call from Kev.

'Right,' Kev said, as I sat down in his car. 'This guy is a bit unsure. You're going to have to be careful.'

'Careful?' I said. 'What do you mean?'

Kev tapped his hands on the steering wheel, as if he was trying to figure out exactly what to tell me.

'We've had a few problems in the past,' he replied.

'Problems?' I said. 'What like?'

Kev inhaled sharply. 'Just don't upset him, right? He gets a bit, well, a bit edgy.'

By now, I was really confused and I wondered what Kev was planning.

'What are you on about?' I said. 'What's wrong with him? And where are we going?'

'We're just going to a restaurant,' he said. 'This guy – well, he wasn't going to take any more girls from me because something happened with Lily Brown and he wasn't too happy about it.'

I started to feel a little uneasy. 'Like what?' I asked.

Kev sighed. 'She wanted more money from him, greedy cow. She started blackmailing him when he wouldn't give her it and it got a bit out of hand. She attacked him with a knife.'

I tried not to look too shocked, but I was quite taken aback. I didn't know Lily, but she'd always seemed quiet at school. Usually, when I saw her shuffling along the corridors, she wouldn't look anyone in the eye, almost like she wanted to blend into the background, like she didn't want anyone to know she was there. I couldn't imagine her going mad and knifing someone, and I didn't understand why she'd be bothered about blackmailing anyone if she had £17,000 sitting in the bank. Surely she could just get on and find some more customers? She was clearly in demand. It didn't really make sense.

'Does Lily still do it?' I asked.

'Oh, yeah,' Kev said, vaguely. 'Sometimes.'

He parked up outside a grim-looking Indian restaurant on a grey, forgotten street on the other side of Telford. Kev pulled the handbrake on, as I tried to peer into the window and catch a glimpse of this man. I probably should have felt scared but I just wanted to get it all over with and get my money.

Kev explained that the man I'd be seeing was from Bangladesh, but his English was good. We walked through the door and the smell of the curries wafted into my nostrils. The ground floor of the restaurant was a grubby little takeaway, with a grease-smeared counter and threadbare chairs where customers could sit and wait for their food – not that there was a sign of any. It was dismal, and a bit like Kev's own takeaway.

Above me I could hear people chatting in a language I didn't understand. There were about four or five Asian men, who all looked to be from Pakistan or Bangladesh, or somewhere like that, and in their late twenties or early thirties. I looked up to see them standing on the stairs. When they saw me, they dropped their voices and started speaking in whispers.

'Come up here,' Kev said, as he led me to the stairs.

As I walked past, each of the men fell silent in turn and I felt really uneasy. I could feel all of their eyes on me, but I just had to ignore them and focus on the money I was going to make.

It was then that I saw the man Lily had attacked. He was tall and thin, with a sleek black bob which was flicked out a little at the bottom. He was wearing traditional clothes, a bit like Mr Khan's.

Wow, I thought. Lily Brown isn't that quiet after all. I didn't give any thought to why she might have attacked him, other than what Kev had told me. It was easier just to accept what he said and get on with it.

'I'll be outside in the car,' said Kev. 'Don't be long.' To the man, he said: 'You can trust her.'

He disappeared down the stairs and the man led me silently to the top floor of the restaurant, where there were lots of tables and chairs but no sign of anyone eating a meal. The lurid purple carpet was horrible and sticky. I wondered where the man might lead me, but he simply took me to the corner of the room.

'Can I trust you?' he asked. His English was good, like Kev had said, but his accent was very strong. I didn't know what to say. I didn't really want a conversation, or a fight. I just wanted to get things over with, take the money and go.

'Yeah,' I said. 'Let's just get on with it. You can trust me.'

He stared at me for a few seconds, as if he was trying to work out whether or not I was telling the truth.

'The last girl Kev brought,' he said. 'She was . . .'

I cut him off. 'I know. But I'm not like her. Let's just do this now.'

He shrugged. 'Take your trousers off, quick. We need to finish before my boss gets back.'

I stepped out of my jeans and he started to touch my breasts over my clothes. He lay me down on the sticky carpet and climbed on top of me, his cream trousers at his ankles. As he started to have sex with me, I could hear a low murmur of chatter from a few yards away. I tilted my head as far as I could to see the other four men standing on the stairs, eyes wide, watching as their colleague had sex with me.

Watching as their colleague had sex with a fourteen-year-old girl.

Despite being worried about his boss returning, this man took a lot longer than the others, and it was horrible thinking of all the others on the stairs watching me. It was one thing having sex with an older man whose name I didn't even know; it was quite another having an audience. I just felt glad he'd only insisted I take my trousers down and I wasn't stark naked.

But even back then I remember thinking that it was hardly the kind of thing that dreams were made of. I wondered just how many times Lily Brown had had to do this to get her £17,000. Maybe that's why she'd got so wound up.

After a couple of minutes, I managed to zone out and ignore the spectators. I just gazed straight ahead at a stack of chairs in the corner of the room and tried to think about anything other than what I was doing. Eventually he finished and handed me two hundred and twenty-five quid, because he hadn't used a condom.

I was playing Russian roulette. At the back of my mind, I knew how easily I could have got pregnant but I chose to live in denial. It didn't bear thinking about, so I simply didn't. It would be another few weeks before I'd even go for the morning-after pill for the first time. Pregnancy was too big a problem for me to contemplate so, in those first few weeks, it was easier to ignore it than to comprehend what would happen if I was caught out.

None of the waiters said a word as I counted the notes carefully, making sure there was exactly two hundred and twenty-five quid there. I shuffled back downstairs, eyes to the ground, as I made my way into the cold evening air and back into Kev's car.

I handed him the pile of notes and he snatched them off me, angrily. I wasn't sure what I was supposed to have done.

'For fuck's sake,' he said. 'That was half an hour you were in there! Don't you listen to a fucking word I say?'

He punched the steering wheel in rage and counted the cash, checking several times that I'd not come back short.

'What?' I said. 'What am I supposed to have done?'

'I told you to hurry up!' he seethed. 'You stupid cow. It's gone seven. Lisa will be fucking fuming at me. I'm already late. Don't you know I have things to do?'

'I don't know what else I could have done,' I protested. 'He just took much longer than the others.'

Kev didn't even look at me as he started the car. We'd been driving for a few minutes when he spoke again.

'It's your fucking job to make sure they don't take that fucking long!' he shouted. 'Didn't I teach you anything? Watch some fucking films, Holly. Be an actress. Do the kind of things that will make *sure* he doesn't take that fucking long! Do you get it?'

I sat back in the passenger seat, feeling a bit deflated. The only way I could get through having sex with strangers was by zoning out, but now Kev wanted me to pretend I was having the time of my life. As we stopped at some traffic lights, he pulled on the handbrake with an almighty jerk and I lurched forward.

'The stupid cunt didn't take Viagra, did he?' he asked me. 'Well, answer me! Did he?'

'I don't know,' I replied, honestly. 'I wasn't gone that long, Kev. Why are you being like this?'

'Fuck this,' Kev said. 'You'll have to learn. Now you're going to have to come to Lisa's with me. I don't have time to fuck about.'

We turned onto the motorway, barely saying a word as he sped down the road, signs flashing by, until he turned off at the junction for Lisa's. Just before we got there, without any warning, he pulled onto the hard shoulder. He didn't say a word as he slammed on the brakes and jumped out of the car, leaving me alone in the passenger seat.

For a moment, I wondered if he was going to leave me there, as I watched him tear up the grassy verge and out of sight. I'd already been abandoned by Mr Khan, so it seemed possible that Kev could do the same, especially as he seemed so mad. I wondered what I would do, as I couldn't exactly walk home along the M54. But what would people say if they found me in an abandoned car on the hard shoulder? How would I explain that one to Mum?

I needn't have worried. Two minutes later, Kev came running back down towards the car, clutching a massive bush he'd obviously ripped from the earth. It was covered in lots of little purple flowers. They looked like violets, but I couldn't be sure exactly. It was the most bizarre sight.

I gazed at Kev in bemusement, as he threw the uprooted bush into the back and little flecks of soil landed all over the seat. He jumped back into the driver's seat and turned back onto the main carriageway, as if what he'd done was the most normal thing in the world.

'What are you fucking staring at?' he said, as my eyes travelled from him, to the bush, and back again. 'Never seen flowers before?'

'Why have you got them in the car?' I asked.

He sighed. 'Well, Lisa wants fucking purple flowers for the

garden, doesn't she? Won't stop going on about it. Maybe this will shut her up. She won't stop moaning at me for missing Saif's bedtime. I'll be fucking blaming you this time.'

He turned off the motorway and we drove along the main road for a few minutes, before he turned into Lisa's street and swung the car into her driveway.

'I'll give you your money now,' he said. 'But you're only getting half. Thirty quid.'

He pulled three crumpled ten-pound notes from the pile I'd given him and stuck out his hand.

'But that's not fair!' I cried. 'Thirty quid! I didn't even do anything wrong.'

'Listen, Holly,' he replied. 'You kept me waiting. And I don't like to be kept waiting. So you'll learn the hard way if you have to. Thirty quid. That's it.'

I didn't know what to say as I took the notes from him and carefully folded them in my purse. I followed him as he pulled the bush with the purple flowers out of the back seat and opened Lisa's door.

She was immaculate, as always, as she stood in the hall-way, arms folded, looking pissed off. She was wearing a long, floaty white skirt and a pink blouse that matched her trademark nails and lipstick. She had super-high wedges on, but they were different from the pair she'd been wearing the first time we'd met.

'Got you something,' Kev said, holding the bush.

Her sneering expression softened a little. 'OK, OK, Kev,' she said. 'You do know you're late, don't you?' She paused for a moment. 'Oh, but it's pretty, isn't it? I do love purple flowers.

But leave it outside. I don't want all that dirt being trodden through the house. I've just hoovered.'

I stood in the doorway, feeling uncomfortable.

'Oh, hello, Holly, love,' Lisa said. She was smiling now. 'Come on in. Can I get you a cup of tea, babe?'

9

Secret Slave

I suppose you might wonder why I kept going with Kev. He didn't threaten me like Mr Khan. He never claimed he'd go after Mum or my sisters if I didn't turn up to meet him. Some people might think I should have just ignored him, blanked his calls and tried to get on with my life. If only it had been that easy.

Kev scared me. He got really, really angry when things didn't go his way. It was almost like he didn't have to make those threats to keep me in line. He knew that if he shouted at me enough, I'd do as he said. This also might sound silly, but it was hard not to do as he said because he was an adult and he had kids my age. He was probably the same age as Dad or Phil. I just felt I had to do what he wanted because he had some sort of authority over me.

It took a while for my family to notice things weren't quite right. I became an expert at hiding my new life from Mum and Dad and Phil, and I was good at it. Very quickly, I adapted to my messed-up double life.

For a start, my grades never once slipped at school. It sounds a bit sad, but school was often the highlight of my day. It was a safe haven and I felt like no one could touch me there. I suppose it helped that Carly wasn't at my school, and neither were any of the boys who taunted me on the street. Now, it seems like a minor miracle, but very few of my classmates seemed to know about my new-found reputation. I had a nice little group of friends, who often asked me why I was never free in the evenings, but I always mumbled an excuse about having to baby-sit my sisters or do my homework, which they seemed to accept. I still think of them and of how utterly gobsmacked they'd have been if they'd known what I was really up to when they were swapping nail varnishes and still going to the underage discos at the snooker hall, never doing more than snogging a boy.

I still loved my travel and tourism class best of all my lessons. There were only around eight of us who'd chosen to do it as a GCSE and we all got on really well. Needless to say, none of the others had a clue about my warped double life – not even the two Asian lads. Our little class felt really safe and cosy but, at the same time, it was the only place I could truly escape, as I learned about lots of far-off places – places hundreds of miles from Telford and the Wrekin and Kev and Mr Khan. When the bell rang to signal the end of the lesson, I always felt a bit sad at having to snap back into the real world. Not that I ever let on how much I really enjoyed it, as I didn't want to seem uncool.

I guess I still dreamed of being an air hostess, but I only allowed myself to think about travelling the world when I was in the confines of that little room. Most other times, the future just wasn't on my radar. Living day to day – hour to hour, even – was hard enough.

One day, travel and tourism had just finished and I was walking through the corridor on the way to my maths class when one of the boys in my year grabbed my arm and beckoned to his mates. His name was Dave and he was a right loudmouth.

'Hey, Holly,' he said, as a small group of spotty teenage boys gathered around him. 'Is it true you give out blow jobs for a tenner?'

Jenny was standing beside me and she burst out laughing as my face burned scarlet.

'Ha!' she said. 'What a load of shit! Why would you even say that?'

Dave looked at me, waiting for a response. I felt frozen to the spot. It was the moment I'd been dreading. If everyone at school had sussed what I'd been up to, I'd be ribbed mercilessly there, too, and every boy in my year would think I was fair game. School was the only place where I could blend into the background, the only place where no one called me a slag. I just couldn't cope with that being snatched away from me.

'Dickhead,' I said, with as much conviction as I could. 'Who'd give you a blow job anyway?'

Jenny grabbed my arm and giggled and, to my relief, Dave's mates laughed too. He looked a little sheepish at my comeback. No one at school ever mentioned blow jobs to me again.

At home, I think Mum was so harassed with bringing up five kids and working full time that she didn't pick up on the subtle signs of what was happening to me. I don't blame her, because I worked so hard at keeping the truth hidden.

My nights were planned meticulously. Mr Khan would pick me up on my way home from school or, shortly after I'd got home, he'd call and order me to meet him. I'd be gone about an hour and I'd get back just before Mum came in. Then, I'd usually do my homework and have my dinner before Kev would summon me out. I'd tell Mum I was just going out with Carly and she never had any reason to doubt me. Kev hadn't yet started to push the boundaries, to keep me out later and later. I was always back by around half-nine and tucked up in bed in plenty of time for a good night's sleep before school.

The changes in my behaviour were very slow and subtle. I'd once had a great relationship with Phil, laughing at all of his jokes, no matter how bad they were. Now, I bit his head off at every turn, especially if he dared try to criticise me for always being out.

'Don't you think you should stay in tonight, Holly?' he said. 'You're always out. You treat this place like a hotel and it's not acceptable. Your mum could do with some help with the girls.'

This made me mad, even as Amy looked at me pleadingly, all cute in her pink pyjamas, as she waited to be carried up to bed. I could tell she found it confusing that I went out more and more but, as much as I loved her, it was the least of my worries. If I didn't keep going out, God knows what would happen to her. I had to keep going. I had to protect her, and Lauren, and Gemma, and Mum, and everyone else who meant anything to me.

'Just leave me alone!' I snapped. 'You're not my dad! You can't tell me what to do. They're your kids. You had them, you deal with them.'

Phil's face was like thunder. 'Do you know how hard your

mum and I work to support you all? Do you know how hard it is for her, trying to work full time and look after you and do all the housework? You never lift a finger, Holly, and neither does Gemma, come to think of it. You swan in and out without so much as helping wash some dishes. Well, that has to change.'

I wanted to slap him, I really did. I couldn't believe he was making such a fuss over some dishes. A pile of dirty plates and cups seemed like the least important thing in the world to me.

'Leave me alone!' I snapped back. 'You heard what I said. You're not my dad.'

I grabbed my coat and slammed the door behind me, as I raced to the end of the road and jumped into Kev's car, just in time to speed off to meet the Chinese man at his posh house on the other side of town. It was a Tuesday, after all.

As for Mum, I think she thought my mood swings were just typical teenage stuff. Gemma had been a bit the same a few years before and nothing terrible had happened. She'd just grown out of it.

Weirdly, it was Lauren and Amy who first started to notice things. Slowly but surely, I could feel our relationship starting to change. I still loved them both to bits, but I knew they were upset that I spent so much time going out and I hardly had any time to play with them. Amy became especially clingy whenever I was at home. We'd always been close and she must have sensed something was wrong, even though she was just a toddler. It's funny how children are sometimes more intuitive than adults.

It all came to a head one day when I left my phone lying on

the coffee table for just a fraction of a second. I'm not sure why I took my eyes off it, even for a moment, as I was always so protective of it. If Mum had read through my texts or looked at my call log, she'd have been extremely suspicious – even though I'd been savvy enough to give people like Kev and Mr Khan code names, so it looked like it was simply other girls in my class who'd been phoning me. Even Beaver, who still called occasionally, despite his terrible English, had an alias.

But Amy knew that every time she saw me on my phone, I'd soon disappear, so she hid it in her toy box. For an hour and a half I searched the house high and low, in absolute hysterics. I was terrified, both that Mum would find the phone and work out what I'd been doing, but also that Mr Khan or Kev had been trying to get hold of me. If I'd ignored them, who knows what the consequences would be?

'Where the hell is my phone?' I roared. 'Where is it? I have to find it and I have to find it now!'

'Why are you so upset, Holly?' Mum asked. 'It must be in the house somewhere, we'll find it. It's not the end of the world, being without your phone for five minutes.'

But there was no consoling me. I was crying so hard I could hardly breathe, choking out big throaty sobs that made my chest heave. Lauren had turned round from the TV programme she was watching and was looking at me like I'd gone mad. Mum obviously thought it was a typical teenage tantrum – that I'd perhaps been texting some boy in my class who I had a crush on – and continued half-heartedly trying to calm me down while she wiped down the kitchen worktops and kept an eye on the girls.

Eventually a distressed-looking Amy grabbed me by the hand and led me to her toy box in the corner of the living room, where she fished it out.

'Sorry,' she said, with a little forlorn look.

'Amy!' I cried in frustration, as I noticed a missed call from Kev from half an hour beforehand. 'Don't ever take my phone again! This isn't a stupid game.'

Mum had come back into the room and she folded her arms. 'Holly, she's just a child,' she said angrily. 'She was just playing. There's no need to speak to her like that. Apologise to your sister, now.'

But I was already racing towards the front door. 'You just don't understand, any of you,' I said, as tears sprang to my eyes again. 'I'm going to Carly's.'

Of course, I wasn't going to Carly's. I practically ran to the end of the street and jumped straight into Kev's car, as he bollocked me for keeping him waiting for so long.

'I'm sorry,' I said. 'My sister took my phone and hid it in her toy box. I was looking for it everywhere.'

I caught sight of my reflection in the wing mirror. My face was still blotchy and tear-stained, my eyes red from crying. The mascara I'd slicked on before school in the morning had gathered in little puddles above my cheeks. I wasn't sure if Kev noticed. If he had, he certainly wasn't going to ask me what was wrong. I quickly dabbed at my face while Kev swore at me and called me a bitch and warned me not to waste his time.

'I'm sorry,' I said, robotically. 'It wasn't my fault. My sister hid my phone.'

I was already feeling a little nervous, as I'd come on my

period that morning. I guessed I wouldn't be any use to Kev, but I figured I'd better turn up anyway and explain my situation to him, just to keep the peace. In a way, I was secretly relieved. I wasn't really in the mood for being pimped out and it was the perfect excuse. Or so I thought.

'Well you're here now, I suppose,' Kev said. 'We might as well get going. You need to keep your phone away from your fucking little sister. I don't want this happening again.'

I nodded. 'OK. But I can't really do anything today anyway, so it doesn't really matter.'

I could see the fury in Kev's deep brown eyes. 'Oh, and why not? This better be fucking good, Holly. I've got two guys waiting for you. We're already late.'

I shifted uncomfortably in my seat as he jolted to a halt at a red light and my seatbelt chaffed against my neck.

'Because I've got my period,' I explained. I blushed a little as I said it. It was weird talking to a guy about that kind of stuff, especially an older one.

I'd been working, if you can call it that, for Kev for nearly three months at this stage, but he still hadn't managed to catch me on my period. I was still quite young, so they were fairly irregular. I expected Kev to explode with rage, to somehow blame me for not being able to control my menstrual cycle. But he simply opened his glove compartment and produced two neat little washing-up sponges, which he'd cut into perfect cylinders. He'd also cut out the middle bit, so they were hollow.

'Well, here you go,' he said. 'Take them. That'll sort you out.'

I looked at them in confusion, as Kev shook his head in

disbelief. 'This happens all the time,' he sighed. 'Just shove one of those up yourself and, you know, problem solved.'

I took the sponges and studied them for a moment, still not quite sure how they worked.

'They won't feel a thing,' Kev said. 'They won't even know, trust me. Just pull it out afterwards but make sure they don't see you doing it. I don't want them asking for any money off because of this – what will we say – *situation*.'

I was stunned. Kev really had thought of everything but, again, he was so experienced. It took me a little while to realise that I was probably his main source of income at that time. Sure, he had his takeaway, but it was always really quiet and he never seemed to be there and the food looked pretty bloody unappetising. What was the point, when he was making hundreds of pounds a week selling me? Still, I could tell he was anxious to make sure he got every possible penny he could. After all, he had a wife and two girlfriends to support, not to mention countless children.

'Oh,' was all I could say. 'Oh. Right.'

I was surprised when Kev pulled up at a takeaway just a few yards from his own. It seemed a bit close to home. Didn't he worry that people would recognise him round there and realise what he was up to? But just like he hadn't been fazed when he'd taken me to the house next to his own, he parked the car and led me inside, as bold as brass.

It's funny how many takeaways I was taken to that seemed to have strange opening hours. Often they'd be closed when we appeared, usually in the early evening, when you'd expect them to be busiest.

This place was the same. Now, I can't even recall what the shop floor looked like, because I was led straight to a godforsaken bedroom at the back. It was tiny, but there were two single beds at each side of the room. There was no other furniture, just two small piles of clothes next to each bed. The window was covered not by a curtain or a blind but by a large piece of discoloured white cloth that looked like it had been hanging there for years. There were spiders' webs dangling from the ceiling and little spots of mould flecked the beige walls. The smell of damp and sweat, mixed with the greasy aromas from the shop just a few feet away, was overpowering.

I'd barely taken in my surroundings when two Pakistani men entered. The first was an older man, probably in his mid-fifties. He was one of the oddest-looking people I've ever seen. He had a huge, bulbous head, with the thinnest covering of jet-black hair, which made him look a bit like an alien. His teeth were horrific and stained dark brown. There were big gaps between them and quite a few were missing. He started to speak and his voice sounded really funny, too. It was squeaky and high-pitched, like it didn't really belong to him. He told me, in his broken English, that he was the chef but I didn't really care. I didn't want to know a single thing about him. I just wanted to do what I had to do and get the hell out of this pokey, smelly room.

The second man was much younger. He was really well built, over six feet tall, with a broad, muscular body. I already felt apprehensive, thinking of his weight on top of me, as he towered over me. I remember thinking how small I felt as I stood next to him and realised that he could actually really hurt me, if he wanted to. I hoped he didn't, and that, like the rest of them, he was just after a quick, cheap thrill.

'We're going to do a deal,' Kev said. 'Tonight you're doing two for the price of one.' His voice dropped to a whisper. 'Don't forget the things I gave you in the car.'

Instinctively, I said, 'No! That's not fair.'

Kev grabbed my arm with just enough force to make me inhale sharply. 'Holly,' he said. 'It's Saif's birthday next month. I'm flat out. Lisa's asked me to get him a million and one things. These guys work here for next to nothing; they can't afford my normal rates but we don't have anyone else tonight. You'll do what you're told.'

I felt pain shoot through me as my stomach cramped. 'Do I have to, Kev? I told you I'm on my period.'

Kev's fingers were still digging into my arm. 'Look, Holly,' he said. 'Do you want me to tell your mum what you've been doing? The sooner you do it, the sooner you can go home.'

It was the first time he'd mentioned Mum to me, and it knocked me off guard big time. Now it wasn't just Mr Khan who was claiming he'd tell Mum, it was Kev too. He must have seen the horror on my face. He didn't need to say a single word more.

'Where's the loo?' I asked quietly, and he led me out to the corridor between the room and the shop, pointing to a door on the left.

It was tiny, with just a little cracked sink and a toilet that looked like it had never been cleaned. It made my stomach turn to think that most of the people who used it probably made or served food. I wondered if this was it, if it was the only bathroom these men had. Their room certainly smelled like they didn't take many showers.

As I held the sponge, I thought about Kev's threat to tell Mum. It didn't for a second occur to me that he'd never do it, because Mum would most likely have gone to the police and his whole sordid little business would have been history and he'd probably have ended up in jail. All I could think of was how scared I was that he'd start threatening to hurt my family, just like Mr Khan had, but he didn't have to. He'd seen the fear in my eyes when he'd threatened to out me, and that was enough to keep me in line.

I took out my tampon and replaced it with the sponge. It felt a bit weird, but I tried to console myself with the fact it wouldn't be in for long. Then I crept back into the bedroom. Kev and the old chef had disappeared and the younger man was sitting on the bed in his pants. The first thing I noticed was that there was a big hole in the side of them.

He pinned me to the bed without a word, and his sweaty, stale smell filled my nostrils as he entered me. It was painful but, as always, I knew I had to try my hardest not to show my discomfort. If I'd thought the Bangladeshi man in the other restaurant had taken his time, he had nothing on this one. I stared at the cracked, mouldy ceiling for what felt like hours, as he kept going and going and going. Every time I hoped it was over, he'd somehow manage to carry on. By the time he'd finally finished, I was in real pain and I winced as he climbed off me without saying a word.

I ran to the little toilet and took the bloody sponge out, replacing it with the second. It was only when I went to walk back to the bedroom that I realised I was wearing nothing but my underwear. For the first time, I hadn't given my modesty a second thought. It was like I'd become braindead.

I lay back down on the bed as the second man came to me. He looked a bit pathetic, with his wrinkly little body and huge, misshapen head. I had to hold my breath as he climbed on top of me. His breath and body odour were both terrible, enough to make me retch. I tilted my head as far away from his face as I could and batted him away when he tried to kiss me.

'No,' I said, as firmly as I could.

He didn't protest, he just forced himself inside me and started to have sex with me. The first man had taken so long that I was really, really sore down there and every move he made was agony. Thankfully he didn't take half as long, but it still felt like ages. I was so relieved when he finished that I jumped from the bed and threw my clothes back on. I'd been in there for ages, so I was dreading what Kev would have to say.

I pushed the door open to see Kev walking out of the deserted kitchen, his hands full of vegetables. I couldn't help but detest him in that moment. I'd been in that horrible bedroom, having sex with those horrible men, and he'd been in the kitchen, stealing vegetables.

I think that was the first time I felt like I really, really hated him.

I was still in lots of pain as we drove home and, as he dropped me at the end of my road, I noticed it was almost ten o'clock. He tossed some notes in my direction, but for the first time I didn't really care how much he'd given me. I wasn't sure I believed they'd only paid half price, but I wasn't even that bothered. The money didn't really mean anything now because, whatever I bought with it, Mum would notice. I'd just hide it under my floorboard with the rest of the cash.

'Holly!' Mum called, as I walked through the front door. 'Have you done your homework? You're in a bit late, are you not?'

I mumbled an excuse about losing track of time because my phone battery had died. I went straight to the bathroom and splashed some water on my face as I gazed at my reflection in the mirror. I didn't look any different to how I had done just a few months earlier, yet I was different. Very different. I was a slag now, or so I thought. No one would ever think of me as being anything else and I'd never be able to escape this. I'd just have to accept it. It was all my fault – for being greedy and taking Mr Khan's money and takeaways and dreaming of making £17,000.

It seemed so silly now. I was petrified Mum would spot a few twenty-pound notes I'd hidden under a floorboard in my room. How the hell would I hide £17,000 from her? I climbed into bed and pulled the covers over my head but I was still feeling uncomfortable and it made it hard to sleep.

The next day dawned and I headed to school as usual. It was a strange feeling. Most teenagers would be counting down the minutes until home time, desperate to be free of classes and teachers. I, on the other hand, wished the day would last forever. As I sat in my IT class, the last class of the day, I could feel the horrible knot of dread tightening in my stomach, as I knew it would soon be time to see Mr Khan.

I grew to hate the sound of the shrill school bell. As it rang out that day, I wearily picked up my books, one by one, wondering just how long I could postpone the worst part of my day.

'We're going to head into town and have a look around the shops,' Jenny said. 'Do you fancy coming?'

'Oh, I can't,' I said. 'I have to look after Amy. And then I'm seeing Carly. Sorry.'

Jenny shrugged. 'OK. See you tomorrow.'

As she and my other friend, Joanne, walked down the stairs of the English block, arm in arm, my heart ached. I longed to go shopping with them, to look at clothes I previously couldn't have afforded. The irony was, I now had so many notes stashed under my floorboard that I probably could have afforded a nice new top, or a pair of shoes. I just didn't have the time, or the energy, to go looking for them.

I managed to walk home that night before my phone buzzed with the inevitable call from Mr Khan. I quickly changed out of my school uniform into some loose-fitting linen trousers. Somehow it always seemed much worse being with him while I was wearing my uniform.

I met him on the main road and he drove out to the Wrekin, where we parked up in a secluded part of the car park, in a little lay-by, away from the other vehicles.

'I will fuck you now,' he said, evil burning in his horrible eyes.

'You can't today,' I began, nervously. 'I'm on my period.'

It was like he hadn't heard me. 'You fuck me,' he said, 'or I will set your house on fire.'

I shook my head, desperately. 'But, no, you don't get it. I can't. I've got my period.'

Mr Khan just looked at me for a few seconds, drumming his long fingers on the steering wheel. I could feel my heart hammering in my chest. It always made me anxious when he threatened my family. Now he was saying he wanted to set my house on fire and I believed he was capable of it. But what could I do? I didn't even have any of the little sponges Kev had given me the night before.

Eventually, he said, 'Prove it.'

'Prove it?' I echoed. 'But how? I'm on my period, I promise you.'

He shook his head and let out a callous chuckle. 'You lying bitch. Prove it.'

I didn't know what to do, so I just sat there, panic-stricken, frozen to the seat. Mr Khan reached over and yanked at my hair, pulling it so hard I let out a little yelp. Then he grabbed hold of my waist and turned my body round to face him. Without a word, he shoved his hand into my knickers and his sneering expression changed in an instant. As he pulled it back, it was covered in blood. My blood. He looked utterly disgusted.

'Dirty bitch!' he hollered. 'You fucking whore, you dirty bitch!'

I swallowed the lump in my throat. 'I tried to tell you,' I said, softly.

'You fucking bitch, you whore!' he said, again. 'Dirty fucking bitch. Get out.'

He leaned over and pushed the passenger door open and practically shoved me onto the stony ground below. I stumbled, but I just managed to regain my balance as I got out. Mr Khan was furiously wiping his bloodstained hand on the seat, the look of disgust still etched on his face. I thought he was going to ask me to go and find something for him to clean it with properly, though what he'd suggest I didn't know, as we were in the middle of nowhere, miles from any shops, and I didn't have any tissues on me.

But before I could get my bearings, he sped off, his Nissan tearing off into the distance. I stood there for a few seconds, naively convinced he would come back.

It must have been a minute or so before I realised he had no intention of returning for me. He'd dumped me again, but this time I'd done nothing. I'd simply had the audacity to have my period.

By now, it was autumn and the nights were getting longer. The sun had already started to set over the big hill and I felt a little scared as I realised I'd have to make my own way back home in the twilight. It would take nearly an hour, by which time it would be pitch-black.

It was then the tears came. I hadn't cried properly in ages, because I'd just been so numb, but now I was scared. Really scared. I was in the middle of the wilderness, completely alone. Anyone could hurt me here and no one would hear my cries. Salty tears splashed down my face and onto my neck and I realised I had no choice but to start walking.

As I trudged along the grassy path, I felt more alone than I ever had in my life. This was it now. This was my life. I was at the beck and call of these horrible men and they'd abandon me without a second's notice. I had no control over them, no control over anything.

As I sobbed softly, the cool October air on my wet face, my phone started to ring. It was Beaver, the man who'd showed me his bits just a few yards from where Mr Khan had dumped me. Although he called often, I could never really understand a word he said. His accent was so thick and he barely knew a word of English.

'Hello?' I said, trying to disguise the despair in my voice.

Beaver started to speak and I was pleasantly surprised. His English was far from perfect but it had improved loads since the night I'd met him.

'Come and meet me now?' he asked.

Suddenly I had a brainwave. 'I can meet you now if you like,' I said. 'But you'll have to come and pick me up.'

Beaver

I was standing by the roadside, about half a mile from the Wrekin, when Beaver drew up in his car. I suppose I should have maybe been a little wary – he'd already exposed himself to me, after all – but I was so relieved that I didn't have to walk all the way home that I just jumped in. He was playing Asian music on the radio and he smiled, exposing his distinctive teeth, as I slid into the passenger seat.

'Hello, Holly,' he said. I nodded by way of response. It had only been a few months since we'd first met but so much had happened that it felt like years had passed. The car was warm and, on the back seat, there was a pile of takeaway pizzas. Beaver had obviously found a job as a delivery driver.

I pulled my phone out of my pocket and sent a text to Mum, telling her I was going to Carly's for dinner. She texted back, saying something about how I'd been out a lot that week already and shouldn't I come home for once? But I just ignored it. I imagined Phil had been kicking off again about how I was never in and I couldn't deal with the hassle.

I expected Beaver to drive me back to Telford, so I was surprised when he turned the car back in the direction of the

Wrekin. Maybe I should have been scared, but I wasn't. For some reason I felt weirdly safe with him. He just seemed a bit bashful and silly. I didn't think he could really do me any harm and I was just glad not to be walking home alone in the dark.

Beaver parked up and, in his broken English, asked where I'd been and who I'd been with. For a moment I thought I might cry again, as I described Mr Khan and how he'd abandoned me, but I managed to hold it together.

'He has sex with me,' I said. 'Nearly every day. And I don't like it.'

I said the words slowly, hoping Beaver would understand what I meant. It sounds strange now, but I couldn't bring myself to use the word rape, because I still didn't feel like a victim. I still blamed myself for what was happening because I'd taken Mr Khan's money and allowed him to buy me a few takeaways. It would be a long, long time before I'd be able to accept that he was abusing me, even though I hated every minute I spent with him.

Beaver shook his head. 'Stay with me,' he said. 'Don't see him.'

I let out a sad little laugh – if only it were that easy, but Beaver looked so earnest that it seemed almost sweet. He told me that he would protect me, that I could call him instead of going with Mr Khan, and for a moment I really wanted to believe he could save me from all of these horrible men. I didn't give much thought to the fact that he was married, and way older than me. I was desperate for something, anything that could keep Mr Khan away from me, even if only for a short while.

'Come with me,' Beaver said. He gestured to the pizzas in the back and I realised he wanted me to accompany him on his deliveries. I couldn't face going home and getting a row from Mum, for staying out so much, so I agreed.

For the rest of the evening, we drove around Telford together. We tried to chat a bit and I was surprised by how we could make ourselves understood to one another, despite the language barrier. I didn't feel attracted to Beaver – not in the slightest – but he did make me laugh. He kept pointing to things and saying the word in Urdu, asking me to tell him the English version. I felt a bit sorry for him. He told me his wife didn't really understand him and they fought a lot. I figured he was maybe just a bit lonely.

As he dropped me at the end of my road, he told me not to meet Mr Khan anymore. He told me I could phone him whenever I needed anything.

'He is horrible,' he said. 'You stay with me.'

For the first time in weeks, I felt like something good had happened to me. At last I had someone looking out for me, and he didn't seem to want anything in return.

Avoiding Mr Khan was easier said than done, though. Every time I thought about cancelling his calls, his threats rang in my ears. At night, I'd often wake up covered in cold sweat, dreaming he'd set the house on fire, like he promised. The dream was so vivid I could see the flames and taste the thick, black smoke. Other nights, I'd imagine him coming for Mum and Lauren and Amy, dragging them screaming from their beds and then doing to them what he'd done to me. So, most nights I'd meet him after school, and most nights he'd have sex with me, even though he knew there were a hundred places I'd rather have been than lying on the back seat of his Nissan, legs akimbo.

Plus, I still had Kev and all the men he'd lined up for me, and that took up at least a couple of nights a week. I still saw the Chinese man in the posh house every Tuesday while his wife was out, and the really old Chinese man was now a regular, too. He'd started having sex with me, but he didn't last very long and he wasn't very big, so it was bearable. I'd have had sex with him a hundred times if it meant skipping just one day with Mr Khan.

The money was starting to make me feel weird, though. There was never as much of it as I expected, certainly nothing like £17,000. If I took any length of time at all, Kev would take money from my cut. One night, we had to drive to a takeaway a few towns away and he charged me for petrol. This pissed me off because of course it was Kev who arranged all of these meetings, not me. But I didn't protest too much, because the notes just got stuffed under the floorboard and forgotten about. Even looking at the money made me feel dirty and I tried to get rid of it in any way I could.

Carly loved it because I was always trying to palm my cash off onto her. On one of our rare shopping trips, she saw a top she liked in New Look and I bought it for her, straight away, without even thinking. It was thirty quid, which would have been a fortune to me before I'd met Kev. Now it was the perfect way to get rid of some of my sordid earnings.

'Wow!' Carly said. 'Thanks, Holly. That's amazing. I can't believe you just bought me that.'

I shrugged. 'Don't worry,' I said.

I also bought us loads of sweets and crisps and fizzy drinks. I often wasn't in the mood to eat, but Carly always was. By now, she was struggling to fit into her size 18 jeans and we weren't yet fifteen. Rolls of fat escaped from under her T-shirts, and even walking up the hill to the phone box would leave her breathless and red-faced.

'I wish I could buy all of the stuff you buy,' she said, as she unwrapped a king-size Mars bar I'd just bought her, before taking a huge swig of sugary Coke. We were sitting on a wall, legs dangling above the ground. 'Why doesn't Kev ever ask me to do it?'

I tried hard to stifle a sigh. It wasn't the first time I wished I'd been overweight like Carly. Perhaps then Kev and Mr Khan would never have looked at me and none of this would be happening.

'It's not that much fun, Carls,' I said. 'You're not missing much. And he gives me shit money now anyway. He takes the piss.'

Carly looked at me, eyes wide. 'Don't you like it anymore?'

I shrugged. 'Dunno,' I replied, eyes to the ground.

'You said it was easy,' she said. 'You said it only lasted a few minutes and then it was done and you got money.'

'Well, sometimes it's a bit longer than that,' I answered, desperate to change the subject.

'But, still,' Carly said. 'You still get money. You can buy whatever you want.'

'Just leave it,' I snapped. 'I don't want to talk about it twenty-four hours a day. I just do it and that's that. It's not a big deal.'

Carly took another big glug of her drink. 'Fine. No need to bite my head off. I was only asking.'

'Fine,' I said. 'Anyway, do you want to come for a drive with this guy who delivers pizzas?'

Carly looked confused. 'Who's that?'

'Oh, just this guy,' I shrugged. 'He's cool, though. But he looks like a beaver.'

The corners of Carly's mouth twitched a little and soon we'd both started laughing. 'A beaver?' she chuckled. 'Like, really?'

I nodded. '*Really* like a beaver.'

For the first time in months, we dissolved into fits of uncontrollable giggles. It was only when we stopped that I realised I hadn't laughed like that in ages.

'You can't call him Beaver, Carly,' I said. 'Like, you really can't. Don't actually say it to his face.'

As if on cue, Beaver's car slid into view. I opened the door and climbed in the front, while Carly stepped into the back next to the big pile of pizzas.

'Hey, Beaver,' she said. 'I'm Carly. Holly's friend.'

I held the sleeve of my jacket over my mouth so Beaver wouldn't see me giggling, but I think the joke was lost on him.

'Hey,' he said. 'What's so funny?'

I couldn't look at Carly because I knew I'd never be able to stop laughing if I did. For the rest of the evening, we drove around with Beaver as he delivered pizzas all over town. He was playing his Pakistani music really loud, and Carly and I thought it would be funny to make him dance.

'Just do it,' Carly said, raising her hands and wiggling her hips. She looked like a reject from a bad Bollywood movie and I nearly wet myself laughing. 'Do this, Beaver.'

'Why your friend call me this?' he asked me, bemused. 'Why she call me Beaver?'

I giggled again. 'She's just a bit confused.'

Eventually Carly managed to persuade him to dance for us and he was even funnier than she was. He looked so awkward as he bobbed his head to the music and swung his flailing arms in the air. I was laughing so much I could barely breathe.

At the end of the night, he went back to the pizza shop and told us to wait in the car. After about five minutes, he brought out a huge cheese and tomato pizza for us to share.

'Wow!' Carly said. 'This is brilliant!'

From then on, I saw Beaver a couple of times a week. Most of the time Carly came too, but sometimes it was just us. I could only see him when Kev's schedule allowed, but thankfully I usually had a few free nights. It was the only time outside of school that I could have a laugh and not think about all the other things going on in my life.

We had some really funny times with Beaver. Mainly it was just Carly and me taking the piss out of him, which I did feel a bit bad about, but it was hilarious. One night, he was delivering a pizza to a house on the street where the phone box was, and he left the car facing down the hill, with the keys in the ignition. Just as he came out of the house, I let the handbrake off and the car started rolling down the street. Carly and I were in fits of laughter as he chased after us in a complete blind panic. He managed to jump into the front seat and slam on the brakes just in time. He told us how dangerous it was, but we didn't really grasp the gravity of the situation. Another night, a few weeks later, I opened the car door as he was going round a really busy roundabout, near to where you join the M54. Carly and I thought it was really funny, but Beaver was very angry.

'Holly!' he shouted. 'Do that again, you go in the back!'

But at the end of every night, he always brought us a huge pizza with extra toppings – anything we wanted, he said.

Even now, I look back on those times, driving around in his car, as some of the happiest memories of my teenage years. Good times were few and far between, so I clung on to them with all my might when they did come along.

Still, the laughs we had with Beaver were never enough to block out all of the other stuff that was going on, especially with Mr Khan. By now, he was having sex with me almost every day, either at the end of the dirt track or the foot of the Wrekin. My happy childhood memories of these places were all but destroyed. Once he'd finished, he'd always hiss his awful threats to me, reminding me what would happen to my family if I didn't do as he said, so the bad dreams and the daily terror continued. Every time poor little Amy jumped into my arms I felt my heartbeat quicken and my palms become clammy with sweat. How could he threaten to harm an innocent little child? So it was safe to say I thought things couldn't get any worse. Then they did. They got much, much worse.

It was November and the ground was icy. There was a sharp chill in the air, as Mr Khan took me from the street and bundled me into the back of the car, like always. He took me to the end of the dirt track and pinned me to the back seat. It was like every other day, but he seemed angrier, more violent than usual. He yanked at my hair and smashed my head on the window as I cried out in pain.

'Shut up,' he hissed. 'Fucking bitch.'

Then he ripped my trousers down and pushed himself inside of me. It was the same as always, but he did it with such force that pain seared through my whole body and, instinctively, I kicked out. Things seemed to happen in slow motion, as my leg collided with the side of his body and he slowly raised his head, rage flickering in his eyes. I expected him to keep going but he stopped and pushed open the door. My trousers and knickers were still around my ankles, but that hardly mattered. Mr Khan pulled me by the hair again – it seemed to be his favourite move – and threw me out of the car. Trousers still down, I rolled onto the muddy ground as he kicked me, hard, on the side of my body.

For a few seconds I lay on the cold ground, shivering and stunned as he opened the boot of his car and began rifling through it.

As he walked back towards me, I screamed: 'No! Please, please, no!'

Because in his hand was a belt, with a huge cold buckle. He kicked me again, so I rolled onto my back and my T-shirt and denim jacket had ridden up a little.

'Please,' I said, again. 'Please, I'm sorry. I'm sorry.'

He stood over me with the belt in his hand, and for a moment I thought he was just trying to scare me, that he'd relented. But just as I tried to get up, he swung it in mid-air, bringing it down on my naked lower back with all his strength.

'Bitch!' he cried. 'Fucking bitch!'

It was so intense it took my breath away, like I'd been winded, but I barely had time to process the pain before he delivered another blow, and another, and another. Each seemed more agonising than the last, and I thought he'd never run out of steam. Tears pricked my eyes and rolled down my face, as he called me all the insults he could think of: bitch, slag, whore, slut, you name it. And you know what? I believed him. As I writhed around in the mud, gripped by the most excruciating pain I'd ever experienced, I believed I was all of those things. I believed I deserved nothing better but to lie half-naked on the ground and have a strange man beat me black and blue because I'd showed just the slightest flicker of resistance when he began to violently rape me.

Finally Mr Khan seemed to flag. It felt like he'd been whacking me with the belt forever when he delivered his final blow, but it must have been no more than a few minutes.

'Fucking bitch,' he said, as he brought the belt down on me one last time. 'Don't you ever do that again.'

When he stopped, the pain took hold with a vengeance. I doubled up in agony and rolled over in the mud, trousers and knickers still down. For a few minutes, I cared very little about being seen by passers-by in my half-dressed state. I was too consumed by the agony. I didn't have to look at my back to know that the blows had left me with angry, weeping sores, which would only get more painful as the days went on.

I knew Mr Khan was going to leave me there. I didn't even

consider for a second that he'd take me home. Like nothing had happened, he opened the boot and chucked the belt back inside. Without another word to me, he jumped in the driver's seat of his car and sped off out of view.

It took me a few minutes before I could even pull up my trousers to protect my modesty. I could hardly sit up, because every move I made was torture. My legs were covered in mud and stray leaves stuck to my thighs. Eventually I managed to sit up straight and pull my clothes back on. As I did, pain seized me again and I doubled over, breathless and sobbing.

I don't know how I managed to stand up, but somehow I did. I didn't know what to do at first, so I just stood in the middle of the dirt track, my head spinning. I knew I was in no fit state to walk home, so I only had one option, really. I fished my phone from the pocket of my jacket and I dialled Beaver's number.

'Can you come and get me?' I winced. 'Mr Khan has dumped me again.'

He said he'd be there in fifteen minutes, once he'd dropped off a pizza, so I had no option but to stand and wait. Once again, darkness was setting in and I felt scared and isolated. For a moment, I feared Mr Khan would come back and attack me again. Then my mind flashed to my family at home and panic rose in my throat. Had he sped off to hurt them now? What if he'd gone to set the house on fire, like he'd said he would, because I'd disobeyed him? But I couldn't concentrate on anything for more than a few seconds before the pain took hold again and my whole body tensed.

Eventually, I saw some headlights in the distance, as Beaver's car slowly rolled up the dirt track to where I was standing. I opened the door and lowered myself in. I tried to sit back but, as my back brushed the seat, I squealed in pain. The only way I could feel vaguely comfortable was to sit forward, almost doubled in two.

'What's wrong, Holly?' Beaver asked. 'Sit back.'

I shook my head, trying my hardest not to cry. 'I can't. Mr Khan beat me up. He hit my back with a belt. It's so sore.'

With that, I couldn't hold back the tears any longer. I dissolved into throaty, animalistic sobs, as I held my head in my hands. Beaver placed an awkward hand on my knee and then he punched the steering wheel really loudly. When I looked up, his expression had changed and anger was spread across his face.

'He hurt you?' he asked.

I nodded, as another salty tear escaped down my cheek. 'Yes,' I said, softly.

Beaver punched the steering wheel again. 'I'll fucking kill him. The bastard!'

11

Mouldy Rooms and More Men

B eaver was furious that Mr Khan had hurt me – even much more than I thought he'd be. It was almost like he was my dad or something. I didn't think he'd be so protective of me but I guess that in a strange sort of way we'd become quite good friends. It was an unlikely friendship but I was glad to have someone on my side, especially someone a bit older.

'I told you!' he said, as we drove back down the dirt track. 'Stay away from him. He's a bad man.'

I was still crying. 'You don't get it,' I sobbed. 'It's not that easy.'

'I said, don't go near him,' Beaver said. 'But you always do.'

I stared straight ahead at the dark road. I was in too much pain to say much more and Beaver softened when he saw the tears were still rolling down my cheeks.

'I'm sorry,' he said. 'But you are my *jaan*.'

I knew *jaan* must be an Urdu word, but I didn't know what it meant. I didn't even think to ask. Usually when Beaver spoke in his own language I'd quiz him on what the words meant and then I'd tell him the English translation. His English had really come on since he'd started hanging around with Carly and me, and I actually felt quite proud. But today I was too sore for any language lessons. I just assumed it was another word for friend.

As we drove back to Telford, Beaver put on some of his music and started to do his ridiculous, awkward dancing to try to make me laugh. I smiled a little but I just wasn't in the mood. I was too sore to find anything funny. But as we drove along one of the main roads into town we stopped at the traffic lights and I felt my stomach turn over. For a second, I forgot the pain in my back. Bile rose in my throat, my eyes fixed on the car in front of us: Mr Khan's Nissan.

I grabbed Beaver's arm. 'Oh, God!' I cried. 'That's him!'

'In front?' he asked.

'Yes!'

I instinctively covered my face with my hands and started to cry again. I didn't know what I expected Beaver to do but, before I had time to think, the lights turned green and he was like a man possessed. He tore after Mr Khan, getting so close to his car that I thought he was going to cause an accident. We must have chased after him for a mile or so, maybe even two, through dark, forgotten streets in nameless council estates all over town. I felt really anxious, and I kept asking Beaver to slow down, scared of what he might do next.

But all he would say was: 'I'll get the fucking bastard.'

For about ten minutes, I honestly thought Beaver was about to run Mr Khan off the road. I was scared, but it was also weirdly exciting. Perhaps some people will think this is wrong, but as we wound through the streets at breakneck speed, I fantasised that we'd crash and Mr Khan would be killed.

Eventually Mr Khan pulled over into a lay-by on one of the main roads and Beaver screeched to a halt behind him. Both of them jumped out of their cars and Mr Khan's face was contorted with fury.

'What the fuck?' he spat. 'You trying to fucking kill me?'

Beaver looked a bit gormless, but he got right up in Mr Khan's face.

'Holly,' he said. 'Why you fucking touch her?'

Mr Khan just sneered at him. 'Fuck off.'

'You fuck off!' Beaver screamed. 'You fucking touch her again, I kill you!'

As I watched from the car, I wondered what Mr Khan would do next. He was so unpredictable. I expected him to open his boot and get the belt out, to start striking Beaver with it too. But they just stood staring at each other for several seconds before he spoke.

'Fuck off, bastard,' he said. He was laughing. 'I'll do what I want.'

He jumped back into his car and it screeched off, just like it had earlier in the evening, when he'd left me rolling around half-naked on the dirt track. For a moment, Beaver looked like he might follow him again, but he'd disappeared out of sight in seconds. I wasn't sure if I should feel safe or grateful that someone was fighting my corner. I felt a bit pathetic, like I didn't really deserve to be Beaver's mate. Carly and I always took the piss out of him but, here he was, sticking up for me, against Mr Khan of all people.

'I get you some food,' he said, gently.

He took me to the takeaway where he worked and came back

out with a massive pizza. I wasn't really in the mood for food but I thought it was sweet of him, so I picked at a few slices. My back was still so sore that I felt sick. I suppose I should have probably gone to hospital to get checked out, but that would have opened a whole can of worms that I couldn't deal with. For a start, because I was under sixteen, the first thing they'd do would be to tell Mum, and how could I begin to explain why I'd been beaten up with a belt?

When I'd put the leftover pizza back in the box, Beaver dropped me home, right to my front door. Normally I'd have been really worried about Mum seeing me in a car with a man who was at least fifteen years older than me, but somehow I let my guard down with Beaver. He wasn't like the others, he was just a mate. Plus, I was in too much pain to care. I was just grateful I didn't have to walk too far.

'Are you all right?' Mum asked when I got in. 'You look a bit peaky.'

'Fine,' I replied. 'Just tired. I'm going to bed.'

For a second, I thought about telling her, about opening the floodgates and pouring my heart out, but I quickly talked myself out of it. I was still convinced she'd go nuts at me for being such a slag. Because that's what I was, right? A massive slag. I wouldn't be in this mess if I wasn't.

I might have been glad that Beaver had stood up for me at first, but I soon began to realise that it had been a terrible idea. He'd made Mr Khan much, much angrier and much more determined to hurt me. Later that week, he asked me if I loved him. I said yes, even though of course nothing could have been further from the truth. I hated him more than I'd ever hated anyone. But he told me I'd taken too long to answer, so he started to hit me with his shoe. It was sore, but nowhere near as sore as the attack with the belt.

Some days he beat me up really badly, others he barely touched me at all. It didn't matter, though. I was still absolutely petrified of what he'd do next. It was like one big mind game to him, and he loved seeing the fear on my face as I tried to second-guess what was coming next. There were times when I wondered if things would be easier had he just given me a right good hiding every day. Then at least I would know what was coming.

But every time he did beat me up, I instantly regretted thinking that, even for a second. Anything could trigger his rages. Sometimes he brought out the belt. Other times it was a little iron bar. It couldn't have been more than eight inches long but it was absolute agony when he struck it repeatedly against my cold, bare skin.

Soon, I stopped asking what I was supposed to have done. He'd beat me for being seconds late to meet him, for having my period, and even if it took him too long to ejaculate. Everything was my fault, so I just lay there and took it and hoped it would soon be over. What else could I do?

I didn't tell a soul. Not Carly, not Beaver, and certainly not Mum. I was convinced no one would understand and, while I was glad Beaver seemed to have my back, I knew it was pointless to get him to intervene. No one could stop Mr Khan when he flew into a fit of rage. Sending other men to shout at him only seemed to fuel the fire. One thing I noticed was that he always seemed to hit me in places that could easily be kept hidden, like my back, or stomach, or the tops of my legs. I guess he didn't want to get caught, and he knew I was so brainwashed that I wouldn't tell anyone. I just felt pathetically grateful that he hadn't hurt my face, because it was one less thing to explain to Mum, who was finally starting to get suspicious.

One evening, as I told her I was heading out to Carly's, I saw her and Phil exchange strange looks, but they didn't say anything. The next night, we were gathered round the dinner table. For once, I was home in the early evening. As soon as I started to speak, they gave each other that look again and I got really pissed off.

'What are you two looking at?' I snapped. 'What's your problem?'

Mum raised an eyebrow. 'You're talking really funny, Holly. Have you listened to yourself?'

I didn't have a clue what they were on about. 'Talking funny?' I spat back. 'What the hell are you on about now? What am I saying that's so funny?'

Phil cleared his throat. 'It's, well . . . it's your accent.'

Liam was pushing his food moodily around his plate, looking like he'd rather be anywhere else but there, and Amy and Lauren were fighting over a toy in the corner. Gemma was at Dad's, where she always seemed to be these days. I didn't see why I had to get all the grief.

'My accent?' I replied in astonishment. 'What's wrong with my accent?'

Mum dropped her fork and looked at Phil again, like they were trying to figure out what to say to me. Phil gave a little shrug, as if to say go ahead, and Mum pushed her plate away, folding her hands as she did so.

'Well,' she said, clearing her throat. 'We've noticed you've been acting a little strangely lately.'

Phil interrupted: 'You're always out.'

I rolled my eyes. 'I'm just seeing my mates, like everyone else. What's that got to do with you? And what's it got to do with my accent?'

Mum and Phil looked at each other again. 'Have you been hanging around with lots of Asian kids at school?' Mum asked. Quickly, she added: 'Not that there's anything wrong with that, not at all. But you sound a bit, you know . . .' she trailed off.

'A bit what?' I snapped back.

'A bit like you're trying to sound Asian,' she said. I glared at her and she quickly changed tack, adjusting her voice so that it was a little more upbeat and breezy. 'It's actually quite funny, Holly. It's like you're trying to do an impression of someone Pakistani but it doesn't sound quite right so it comes out a bit weird.'

Phil started chuckling, too. I was incensed.

'You're all mental!' I cried, shoving my chair into the table and running upstairs to my room. I flopped down on my bed and pulled my pillow over my head in frustration. If only they knew, I thought. If only they bloody knew.

I hadn't realised that my accent had changed, but it kind of made sense. I spent so much time with people who didn't speak good English, like Mr Khan and Beaver and all of the men Kev took me to, that I guess my accent had just adapted so I could make myself understood. But it made me feel massively self-conscious. I thought about Jenny, and all my friends at school. Had they noticed? Did they think I was a total weirdo? If they'd picked up on it, they certainly hadn't said anything but it didn't stop me worrying.

My train of thought was interrupted abruptly as Kev's number flashed up on my phone. I didn't like answering the phone to him in the house, in case anyone heard, but everyone else was still downstairs so I decided to chance it.

'Hello?' I said.

'I've got some people for you,' Kev said. 'Be at the end of the street in ten minutes.'

I didn't even think twice. I picked up my jacket and walked downstairs, past Mum and Phil, who were still sitting at the kitchen table. I almost tripped over one of Amy's toys and she gave me a sad little look as she saw that I was once more heading out of the house.

I turned away.

Phil stood up, gathering the plates to take them to the sink. I could just tell he was about to say something.

'Before you ask, I'm going to Carly's,' I said. 'It's not a crime.'

Mum turned to me. 'Doesn't Carly's mum get sick of you hanging round there all the time?' she asked. 'Doesn't Carly ever want to come here?'

I sighed. Carly was an only child, so at least I had the perfect excuse. Even though we hardly ever spent any time in her house, it was far less chaotic than mine.

'No!' I said. 'Why would she want to come round here and

listen to you two make up some crap about me sounding like a Pakistani? Plus, it's too crowded here. Hers is way quieter. At least we get some peace there.'

Mum looked a little hurt as I headed out the door, but she was still completely and utterly clueless.

Kev told me we were heading to a takeaway on the other side of Telford. I'd seen so many takeaways that they all seemed identical, and sometimes I couldn't remember if I'd been in the same one twice.

'Oh,' I said. 'You better give me some of those sponges. I've got my period.'

I was a bit surprised when Kev opened the glove compartment and told me just to take all of the sponges there, but I figured he maybe just wanted me to stock up. I shoved them in the pocket of my denim jacket as we drew up outside a grey building. On first glance, it seemed completely indistinguishable from all of the other places I'd been. It was only the tatty, weather-beaten sign that told me it was a kebab house.

We usually went to curry houses or Chinese places, because that's where most of Kev's customers worked. I later discovered that he picked most of them up in a betting shop near Dad's flat. He'd just stand there most of the day, looking for people he thought might be interested in buying an underage girl, after they'd put their coupon on, or had a flutter on the horses. It really was quite sick.

Where Kev had come across these men was the last thing on my mind back then. All I knew was that I'd have to sleep with them. Why bother thinking about their background or who they were? I had absolutely no interest in any of them. I didn't even want to know their names. The only way my brain could cope with what I was doing was to keep them completely anonymous, to avoid eye contact as much as possible. It made my skin crawl when one of them tried to kiss me, or if they tried to have sex with me slowly, like I imagined you might do with someone you actually liked and wanted to be with. To me, that was just a way of making it last longer, and I absolutely hated it. Not that I could say anything, of course. I just had to lie there, silent and compliant.

Just like when Kev sold me to the Bangladeshi man who had been attacked by Lily Brown, there was a huddle of men on the stairs, all whispering and talking in a language I didn't understand. They were Asian, but they didn't look Chinese or Pakistani, and they weren't speaking Urdu or Mandarin or Punjabi, or any of the other languages I'd come to recognise. Their skin was lighter than Mr Khan's and Kev's and Beaver's, so I guessed they must be Turkish, or maybe Kurdish. They were all young compared to Kev, but still way older than me. I figured the range to be from mid-twenties to early thirties, but I didn't even take in any of their faces, as I stood at the bottom of the stairs. I didn't know which one of them wanted to buy me, but it hardly mattered.

'This is the girl,' Kev said, as a hush fell upon the group of men. 'You want her, you pay upfront. Hear that? You want her, you give her the money first, before you do anything. And queue up on the stairs.'

He turned to me before it sank in that he was offering me up to each and every one of them.

He led me to a room at the back of the shop. I expected it

to be much like the room where the chef with the strange-looking head and his younger colleague had slept, but it was much bigger, like a dormitory. There were probably ten beds, none of them made properly. The walls were a dull magnolia colour and, again, the putrid smell of damp was everywhere. Kev pointed at one of the beds.

'Can I go to the loo first?' I asked.

He sighed, remembering my 'inconvenient situation'. 'Well, I guess you better, eh?'

I scuttled down the hall and pushed open a few doors before I found the bathroom. It was so tiny I could touch the door with my legs when I sat down on the toilet. There was no towel and, when I ran the tap, no hot water. There wasn't even any loo roll. I quickly pushed the sponge inside me and walked back down the corridor to the bedroom, where I lay on the bed I'd been shown, fully clothed but waiting.

The first man walked in. I deliberately tried not to look at his face or to take in any of his features. I just looked at the mould-streaked ceiling above me.

'Take your clothes off,' he said. He chucked a pile of notes on the floor next to the bed. I knew I should have counted them, as Kev would be mad if I hadn't got the right amount, but I didn't have the energy.

I faced the wall as I peeled off my top, then my jeans, and unhooked my bra. This man – my first customer of the evening, it appeared – was already pawing at my crotch and pulling my knickers down. I just zoned out as he started doing what he'd paid to do. He wasn't wearing a condom so, as I kept my eyes fixed on the ceiling, I started to wonder how I'd get hold of the morning-after pill the next day. By now, I'd got it ten, maybe fifteen times. It wasn't even a big deal. I always went to the same walk-in clinic and it was usually the same nurse who gave me it. Often, I'd even be in my school uniform but no one ever asked any questions or even tried to tell me about safe sex. I guess if they acknowledged how often I was in there, they'd have to delve a bit deeper and they probably didn't have the time or resources to do that. They seemed to be content with just making sure I didn't get pregnant.

The first man was still having sex with me when the second entered the room. I was a little confused at first but well beyond being embarrassed. By now, it was obvious that he was going to do exactly the same to me in a few minutes. He just lay on his own bed and popped his headphones in, as if we weren't there.

When the first man had finished, he said, 'You can go to the bathroom now.'

I got up off the bed and walked down the corridor, stark naked, past all of the men queuing on the stairs. I'm not sure how many of them there were. Maybe eight, perhaps nine. They looked like they were lining up to get into a nightclub, not to have sex with a fourteen-year-old girl. It was surreal. They all gawped at me as I pushed open the bathroom door but I didn't care. It was like I was in a trance. It's obvious I'm going to have to shag them all, I thought. What difference does it make if they see me naked now, or in ten minutes' time?

I took the sponge from inside me and rinsed it out. I felt a little bit sick, as my blood stained the sink red. It really was disgusting. Still, I put it back in and walked back down the corridor, back to the big bedroom and my next customer.

Every single one of them came to me, one by one, tossing their money down before they climbed on top of me. Often, they'd be only halfway through when the next one in line would come in and lie on another bed, willing it to be their turn. After one man had finished, I'd go off to the bathroom, clean myself up a bit, maybe put another sponge in, and go back to the next.

I felt so empty, like I couldn't feel what was happening, and that I was watching myself from above. It genuinely felt like a weird, out-of-body experience, but I guess that was the only way my brain could cope with what I was doing. I had to completely shut off. My body was there, on that grubby mattress with its thin, dirty blanket, but my mind most certainly was not.

I'm not sure how long I'd been in there when the last one finished, but it must have been at least a couple of hours, as some of them really took their time. When this last guy crawled off me, panting in sick satisfaction, I expected to feel relief – but none came.

Instead, I felt pain. Real searing, sudden, gripping, stomach-churning pain down there, like I'd never had before, not even with Mr Khan. I could tell it would take me days to feel normal again, but I wouldn't get any respite. Tomorrow was Tuesday, so Mr Khan would rape me after school and then I'd have to see the Chinese man with the posh house, as always.

I almost forgot to pick up the money, as I climbed back into my clothes. Most of the men were back in the room now and were talking loudly in their own language. I can't remember their faces, only their voices. I knew they were talking about me – making crude, disgusting comments about my body and how I looked, comparing notes on my boobs and my bum and what it had been like – but I didn't give a shit. I just wanted to get out and get as far away from the kebab shop as I possibly could.

I winced in pain as I walked back out to the car where Kev was sitting with the engine running, and I winced again as I lowered myself onto the passenger seat. I expected him to shout at me for taking ages, but he didn't say a word. He just grabbed the money from me. It was only as he started counting it out that I realised how much of it there was. There must have been well over a grand there, maybe closer to two. I didn't understand how men like that, working in a grubby takeaway, probably for less than the minimum wage, could afford to spend hundreds of pounds on sex, but I didn't want to give it much thought. They'd found the cash from somewhere, hadn't they? Who was I to argue?

Kev tossed me a few of the notes but they sat in my lap for a few seconds before I even picked them up. When I did, I didn't even bother counting them.

How much had I been worth that night? I didn't want to know.

12

Omar

Before I'd yet reached my fifteenth birthday, Kev was making more and more appointments for me and my little stash of cash under the floorboard was growing by the week. I was still terrified Mum would discover it, so I gave it away whenever I could, mainly to Carly, because none of my other friends really knew what I was up to, but sometimes to Beaver, if he was really skint.

I felt a bit sorry for him, really. He told me things weren't going well with his wife. They'd just sort of been thrown together and they hadn't really had any time to get to know each other before they'd got married. Now she was pregnant and Beaver wondered how they'd manage to make ends meet when their baby came along. He delivered pizzas and she worked in Tesco, so they were hardly loaded.

'I'm happy I can talk to you,' Beaver would say, then he'd give me that bashful, toothy grin that made me feel really sorry for him.

One good thing about Beaver, and perhaps even Kev, was that when I was out in their cars with them, I was away from all the local teenage boys who still hassled me and goaded me for blow jobs. Carly and I hardly ever walked to the church now, next to the bench where we'd first met Ali and his mates, and this whole thing had begun. Whenever we did see them on the street, though, they went nuts, constantly asking for blow jobs and other horrible sexual favours. I tried to ignore them, but it was hard.

'Sort it!' they'd always cry. 'Go on, sort it!'

Sometimes, I answered back and told them they were dickheads and they should fuck off, but mostly I ignored them. It didn't stop them calling me, though. I must have got scores of phone calls a day, and texts too, all asking for the same thing. So when my phone rang one December evening with a number I didn't recognise, I felt I knew what was coming.

I decided to answer it. Sometimes I ignored the calls, but sometimes it was easier to pick up or the boys, or men, would just keep hounding you until you did.

'Hello?' I said.

'Hey, is that Holly?' The voice on the other end sounded young and chirpy, but I didn't recognise it. I didn't say anything for a few seconds, as I waited for a crude remark, but none came. 'Are you there?'

'Yes, yes,' I said. 'Who is this?'

'You're going to think this is really weird,' the caller said. 'But my name is Omar. I go to school with your friend Carly. I've seen you around and I think you're really pretty. I'd like to meet up with you. Are you around tonight?'

I immediately felt this was some kind of trap, a trap I'd fallen into before and one I was sure I didn't want to fall into again.

'No,' I snapped back. 'I'm not. I don't even know you.'

'Holly, I honestly don't want anything,' he said. 'I know what people say about you but I don't care. I just want to talk to you.'

'Well, talk to me on the phone,' I retorted.

'Come on,' Omar said. 'Just come and meet me by the church. Please. Just for fifteen minutes.'

I don't know why I decided to say yes. I think it was just because he was the first boy my own age who'd called me up and not asked for a blow job before he'd even said hello. He'd been nice to me and, God knows, I needed someone to be nice to me.

It was early evening and I'd already had a horrible hour in the car with Mr Khan. He hadn't beaten me, but he'd been really aggressive when we'd had sex and he kept saying something about how he'd beat up Liam if I told anyone what was going on. No one in my family was immune, it appeared.

There was a sharp chill in the air and it was too cold for my denim jacket, so I pulled on a big winter coat and started to walk to the church. I was halfway there when my phone beeped with a text from Omar's number.

Meet me next to the bench x.

I felt really uneasy, wondering who would be around the corner and what they'd say to me, but the streets were fairly quiet and, because I'd pulled the hood of my coat up, I didn't attract much attention. It was only as the church came into view that I realised I had no idea what Omar looked like. He could literally have been anyone. I didn't even know for sure he was my age and I half-expected to see a burly man in his twenties standing by the bench as I approached, ready to bundle me into his car and do what everyone seemed to think they had the right to do to me.

So I was pleasantly surprised when I saw Omar for the first time. He was indeed my age and really fit. It makes me laugh now, but I remember my stomach somersaulting as I thought to myself that he looked a bit like Peter Andre, with his floppy black hair, smooth, sallow skin and deep, dark eyes.

'Hey,' he said. He was a little more awkward in the flesh, but I didn't really mind. 'Eh, well, do you want to go for a walk or something?'

I nodded, equally awkward. 'OK,' I said.

We meandered down the street in silence and, for a few precious moments, I felt like a normal teenager. Here I was, with a boy I had a crush on, but neither of us knew what to say to each other. It was strange, really. I was ten times more sexually experienced than any other teenage girl I knew, yet I hardly had a clue how to speak to a boy I liked. I guess, apart from Imran, I hadn't ever really fancied a boy before. I hadn't had the time, or the energy.

My mind flashed back to Imran and how he'd been when we first met – all smooth and chatty, always knowing exactly what to say. In a way, I was kind of glad Omar wasn't confident, otherwise I'd have felt he too was tricking me, and that this was yet another trap to get me to give someone a blow job.

We sat down on a high wall at the end of the street. Omar was the same height as me, and his legs didn't quite reach the ground. They swung in mid-air a little. It was quite sweet, really.

'I know everybody slags you off,' he said, breaking the silence. 'But I'm not like the other boys.'

I was instantly defensive. 'Who slags me off?'

Omar looked at the ground, shyly. 'You know what people say. Don't you?'

I shrugged, sadly. Of course I did. There was no point in denying it.

'Do you actually do all of those things?' Omar asked.

'No!' I gasped, a little too quickly, my cheeks flushing. 'Why? Is that what you want? One of your silly mates started a rumour that I give out blow jobs and now you've asked me here to see if you can get one?'

Omar shook his head emphatically. 'No!' he said. 'I promise you, I'm not like them. I didn't think you did all that. I think you seem nice.' His hand brushed against mine and I felt butterflies swirl around in my stomach. 'Really nice.'

We sat there on the wall, just looking at each other for a few minutes, and giggling a little. It felt so weirdly normal and I wished we could stay there for the rest of the night, until it was time to go home. Above anything else, it was just nice to feel something and not to want to completely switch off my brain and my emotions.

But after a short while, I felt my phone vibrating in my pocket. I took it out to see Kev's number flashing impatiently on the screen and my stomach flipped again, but not in a good way this time.

'I . . . I think I have to go,' I said. 'Sorry.'

Omar looked a bit disappointed. 'Already? We've only been here, like, ten minutes.'

'It's my mum,' I lied. 'She'll go mad if I'm not home soon. I said I'd baby-sit my little sister.'

Omar smiled, revealing his perfect row of gleaming white teeth. He had one of those lovely smiles that lit up his whole face. His brown eyes seemed to dazzle as he looked at me.

'OK,' he said, finally. 'But I'll call you tomorrow?'

I nodded, trying not to look too eager. 'Yes,' I said. 'Well, if you want.'

Then he slowly placed his hand on the small of my back and pulled me close to him. His body felt so warm, compared to the frosty December air. Suddenly he didn't seem awkward or nervous at all. I relaxed, too, as he tilted my face towards his and planted his lips on mine. Slowly and softly, he began to kiss me. It felt nothing like the forceful kisses of Mr Khan or the men Kev took me to, where I clamped my mouth shut and their horrible tongues collided with my lips. It didn't even feel anything like when I'd kissed Ryan at the underage disco, which seemed like a lifetime ago.

I could have stood there in his arms forever but my phone was ringing again and Kev was getting impatient.

Pulling away, I said, 'I'm sorry. I really have to go.'

Omar gave my hand a little last squeeze. 'OK. But I'll call you tomorrow. I promise.'

It was only when he was out of earshot that I dared answer Kev. He sounded impatient and frustrated, as always.

'About time,' he snapped. 'I've been calling you for the last ten minutes. I'm at the end of your road.'

I can't even remember who Kev took me to that evening. I guess it can't have been that bad, in the grand scheme of things, because I'd have probably remembered had it been really horrendous. It sounds bad, but when you're seeing so many horrible men so often, one encounter merges into another and only the really awful ones stick out. I later learned that some girls who were sold like I was were plied with alcohol and drugs as a way of making them comply – of numbing them to the horrors of what they were being forced to do. But I was never given anything, not in the early days, anyway. Nothing to cloud my brain, or to help me forget. It was up to me to close my mind off. I had to block it all out myself and I guess I got quite good at it.

After we'd finished, Kev would often take me to Lisa's or back to the family home, next to the house where I'd first met the really old Chinese man who touched my boobs. No matter what time it was, Lisa would always be dressed to the nines, full of smiles and cups of tea, calling me babe and sweetie and darling and asking how I was, was school busy, had I had a nice weekend?

Every time I saw her smile at me with her perfectly made-up lips, I liked her a little less. At first, I'd been so naive I'd given her the benefit of the doubt. She'd seemed so normal. Surely she'd have felt sick to her stomach if she'd realised Kev was selling young girls to pay for her make-up and clothes and fancy furniture? But the longer things went on, and the more Kev took me to her house on the way to or from some sordid job he'd lined up for me, the more I couldn't accept that she didn't know exactly what was going on. Why didn't she think it was really weird that her forty-something boyfriend kept turning up on her doorstep with a fourteen-year-old girl he appeared to have no connection with?

Lisa knew. She knew all right, but she chose not to say a single word because the money I made for Kev paid for her shoes and her leather couch and her lipstick and the toys for the love-child she'd had with the man who was touting me around town like I was a piece of meat. I still sipped my tea and thanked her politely, because what else could I do? But when she tried to chat to me, my answers became shorter and more clipped and, when we left, I didn't smile as I said goodbye like I used to.

'See you soon, honey,' she'd say, all sugary. She was still pretending to be oblivious to how much I was beginning to resent her but, as I shuffled out of the door, I sometimes looked back and caught her eye. I wanted her to see the torment hidden within me, but she'd always quickly look away. There were times when I wanted to run back up her driveway, past the bush Kev had stolen from the grass verge at the side of the M54, and barge into her house and ask her did she know? Did she know what I'd had to do so she could get those designer wedges or that new phone? But of course, I never did, because what would Kev do then?

Still, sipping tea in Lisa's was preferable to being taken back to the family home. The girls would always stand at the top of the stairs and stare at me wordlessly, like I'd arrived there from another planet. I don't think I ever saw either of them on the ground floor any time I went there, which was really odd. From what I could gather, their mum's health was getting worse and worse and she needed more care. Not that you would have guessed it from the way Kev acted. He never once popped up to see if she was OK, or expressed any kind of concern for her.

Farooq and Imran were still allowed to do just as they pleased. Imran was out all the time with Ali and the other boys, so thankfully I rarely bumped into him. Farooq always seemed to be home, though, and most of the time he'd be watching his porn videos in the lounge. Needless to say, Kev never batted an eyelid. One evening, I was sitting awkwardly on the sofa, trying not to watch him as he masturbated, when he came over to me, boxers round his ankles.

Without warning, he started swinging his penis in my face and rubbing it on my cheeks. I was caught so off guard that I jumped out of the chair, but Farooq didn't give over.

'You like me, Holly?' he sneered. 'You like my dick?'

At that point, Kev appeared in the doorway, clutching a cup of tea and shaking his head with a little chuckle, as if he'd caught Farooq sneaking an extra chocolate bar into his lunchbox. He didn't try to stop him, but Farooq soon got bored and turned back to his film. As the moans of another big-breasted blonde woman rang around the room, he started wanking again.

I think that's maybe why I got so attached to Omar. I hadn't wanted a boyfriend, far from it, but he was an oasis of normality in my very abnormal world. I'd only ever get to see him for twenty minutes a day, half an hour maximum, because I was always on such a tight schedule, so this free time became so precious to me. I'd see Mr Khan after school, then I'd go home and do my homework and maybe grab some dinner. Most nights Kev would pick me up and take me to some filthy house but, if he didn't, Beaver would collect Carly and me and we'd help out with his pizza deliveries. I suppose I didn't really have to see Beaver, because he was just a mate and didn't make any demands, but I wanted to. I felt like he needed us, Carly and me. We helped him with his English and he told us his problems. It didn't seem like he had many other people to talk to and he really wasn't happy at home. I don't think he really wanted to have a baby, but he never said as much.

'You always have to go so quickly,' Omar said one night, as he'd pulled me in for another kiss. 'Can't you stay just five minutes longer?'

'I can't,' I sighed. 'I really wish I could but I have to be home. My mum goes out every Tuesday and I have to look after my sisters.'

'Where does she go?' Omar asked.

Without thinking, I came up with a lie: 'She does a college course. Between half-five and half-seven.'

Omar kissed me again, threading his hand through mine. 'It's ten past. You better go.'

'I'll ring you tomorrow,' I said.

'OK,' he replied. 'Oh, but Holly?'

'Yes?'

'I was just ... you know ... kind of wondering, if you'd maybe ...'

'Maybe what?'

'If you'd maybe be my girlfriend?'

My eyes lit up. 'Yes,' I replied, without hesitating. 'But I really have to go.'

I practically skipped all the way down the road, even though I was heading to Kev's car. It felt totally different from when Imran had asked me to be his girlfriend. This time it felt real. Omar hadn't even asked me for a blow job. He hadn't even mentioned it. He only seemed to want to kiss me.

I was on such a high that I didn't even mind that I was heading off to have sex with an old man. It was only the Chinese man with the posh house. I knew it would be painless and it wouldn't take long and I was right. As I walked back to the car, head still in the clouds, thinking of Omar, I handed the pile of notes to Kev.

As usual, he counted every single one, and then counted them again, to make sure I'd come back with the right amount. When he was satisfied all the cash was there, he started the car and we drove off back in the direction of home. I thought I was done for the night, but I was wrong.

'I've got someone else for you,' Kev said. 'But not now. Later.'

'Later?' I said. 'How much later? I've got school in the morning.'

Kev rolled his eyes. 'Bloody hell, Holly, you can stay out late one night. It won't kill you. Half past ten. I'll pick you up at the end of your road at quarter past.'

It was the first time Kev had ever asked me to stay out that late, but I could tell from his tone of voice that it wasn't an option. Still, I started to panic a little about how I'd explain it to Mum. Plus I'd arranged to meet Carly and Beaver later and I felt a bit bad. Beaver's baby was due in just a few weeks and he was getting more and more anxious about becoming a dad. I felt I had to be there for him.

In the end, I told Beaver I'd meet him the following night and asked Carly if she wanted to come along. I assumed she wouldn't, as she'd have to sneak out too, but she seemed keen. I couldn't think of a decent excuse for Mum, so in the end I decided I was going to pretend I was having an early night, then creep back out, making as little noise as possible. Mum always bathed the girls and put them to bed early, and then she and Phil were usually so exhausted they didn't stay up too late. They'd usually gone upstairs by ten o'clock.

That evening, they seemed to take longer than usual and my heart was pounding in my chest as the minutes ticked round and I could still hear the noise from the telly in the living room below. Quarter to ten came and went, so did ten to. I wondered what would happen if I didn't turn up. Would Kev come marching round to our house and tell Mum I was a prostitute to spite me for messing up his arrangement? I hugged my knees as I let the thought swirl around in my brain, but in the end I had to stop thinking about it because it was unbearable.

At ten o'clock, they still hadn't come upstairs and my palms had started to get sweaty. I could hear the distinctive chimes of the *BBC News at Ten* coming from downstairs and I felt dizzy with frustration. Why are they watching the bloody ten o'clock news? I thought. They never stay up to watch the news!

Just then, my phone lit up with a text message. I grabbed it and opened it straight away, thinking it might have been Kev, fifteen minutes early, without any warning. But it was from Omar.

Night gorgeous. Can't wait to see you tomorrow xxx

I thought about Omar, who was probably tucked up in bed

by now, just like I should have been. But here I was, lying under the covers, fully clothed, waiting for an opportunity to sneak out into the darkness. He had no idea my night was just beginning.

Finally, at five past ten, the sound from the telly stopped and I heard two sets of footsteps on the stairs. Beads of sweat were forming on the back of my neck, as I knew I was on borrowed time. I heard Mum go into the bathroom and start brushing her teeth and washing her face and doing God knows what else. By the time she'd finished, it was twelve minutes past and Phil still hadn't been in yet. He'd just gone in and closed the door when my phone lit up again. This time, it was Kev.

At end of road. Hurry up.

I wasn't sure what to do and I was feeling really panicky. Should I try to sneak out now, really quietly, and risk bumping into Phil on the stairs? Or should I wait a few minutes, until he was done in the bathroom, and they'd put out the bedroom light? I had to make a split-second decision and I decided on the second option. If Phil saw me creeping down the stairs fully clothed, he'd go absolutely nuts and the whole house would be awake and I'd have to sit and listen to a lecture for twenty minutes. If that happened, there would be no way on earth I could meet Kev. My knuckles were white, as I clutched my phone in my hand and tapped out a reply to Kev.

Be there soon. Just trying to sneak out.

The response came within seconds.

Hurry up!!! Need to be there by 10.30.

It was already seventeen minutes past ten when Phil closed the door and turned out the light on the landing, but I knew

I couldn't leave straight away. I had to wait at least a couple of minutes, but those minutes seemed to take forever as the clock ticked by. Kev rang me twice but I ignored it. If I started talking on my phone, someone might hear and then I wouldn't be able to get out.

It was twenty-one minutes past before I decided to bite the bullet and just go for it. Phil was evidently wiped out because I could already hear him snoring loudly from the bedroom. I hoped Mum had fallen asleep just as quickly, or at least that she was dozing off.

I carried my shoes in my hands as I eased down the stairs on my tiptoes, in the dark. I prayed Lauren or Amy hadn't left a toy on the stairs because if I tripped and made any kind of noise, it was game over and I'd be in the shit. I'd been late for Kev before, and missed a few of his calls, but I'd never yet failed to turn up completely and I really didn't want to find out what would happen the first time I was a no-show.

My heart leapt with every tiny creak the stairs made. I remember asking myself why they never normally seemed to make any noise, why they only refused to be silent when you really needed them to be. With every step I took, I was convinced I'd turn round to see Mum or Phil standing at the top of the stairs, absolutely fuming.

I finally reached the bottom and breathed a shallow sigh of relief, but I still had to get out the door. Slowly and carefully I pulled the door handle down and eased myself across the threshold and onto the first of the stone steps outside. I closed the door as softly and as stealthily as I could, and then stood with my back against it for a few seconds, heart hammering wildly.

I was out.

It was only then that I put my trainers on. I began to run, as the cold February rain blew into my face. I didn't even waste time doing up the laces; I just bolted as fast as I could to Kev's car, with its engine running, at the end of the road. God knows what the neighbours must have thought, but none of them seemed to say anything to Mum, or to suggest that they'd seen me.

I practically threw myself into the front seat. Carly was already sitting in the back. It was now twenty-six minutes past and we were really late.

'We'll never make it on time now,' Kev hissed. 'This is a fucking joke. If he cancels, this is all your fault.'

I genuinely thought he might kill us, as he tore through the streets at breakneck speed. He was driving the way Beaver had on the day he'd chased Mr Khan but, this time, I didn't feel like anyone was trying to protect me, so I just felt really frightened. It was only as we swung round a corner and my phone lit up again that I realised I hadn't replied to Omar. He'd texted again.

You OK? xxx

I managed to tap out a quick reply before we parked up behind another nameless takeaway on another nameless Telford street, telling Omar I was fine and that I'd see him the next day. As awful as it sounds, for a moment I kind of hoped Kev would send Carly in and I'd get to sit in the car for once. I didn't want to spend half an hour looking at him as he silently seethed and raged with impatience over the time it was taking for him to get his precious money, but it was better than having to actually go in and do the deed.

But he said: 'Carly, stay there. I'll be back out in a minute.'

I managed to stifle a sigh, as I dutifully followed him up a set of stone steps and into another rank hellhole of a place that had the audacity to serve food and charge people for it. The chef was standing at the top of the stairs, still wearing his white, curry-stained work clothes. He was quite tall, with long black greasy hair that clung to his cheeks. I thought at first he was Pakistani, but I soon figured he was probably Bengali because he didn't speak Kev's language.

'Go into the room,' Kev barked, and I did as I was told. I eased myself onto another filthy, moth-eaten mattress as I took in my surroundings. The room was one of the tiniest I'd ever been in, and there was barely any room for the bed. But hanging above me was a washing line, with six or seven pairs of pants dangling from it. Every single pair had a hole in them but I bet the chef wasn't one bit embarrassed. After all, no one needed to put on airs and graces for a little slag like me, did they?

I could hear Kev and the chef arguing outside in English, talking about money and how much he was willing to pay. He sounded really tight because every price Kev gave, he tried to haggle. I tried not to listen. I didn't really want to know how little Kev was going to let me go for, after dragging me out of my bed in the middle of the night.

They must have eventually struck a deal because the chef soon came into the room and threw his stained overalls on the floor, before tearing at my clothes and unhooking my bra. He was holding a bottle of water, which he tossed down by the bed before climbing on top of me, and then the inevitable began.

At first I just looked straight ahead, at the pants hanging from the washing line. They were a bit disgusting but at least they gave me something to focus on. But twenty minutes must have gone past and the chef seemed no closer to finishing. Twenty minutes became half an hour, and when half an hour turned into forty-five minutes there was a thud on the door.

'Fucking hurry up!' Kev's voice hollered from outside. 'Fucking dick. I haven't got all night.'

The chef – who hadn't yet said a word to me – just laughed. For a moment, he stopped and I wondered if he'd just got bored, so I started to sit up, but he pinned me down again. He took a huge swig of his water and then just spat it on the floor, like he was a child playing in the bath and this was all a big game. Then he started again.

He'd been inside me for about an hour and a half when I started to feel really sore. I didn't just hurt down there. The tops of my legs were aching from bearing his weight and I was really, really tired. All I could think of was how exhausted I was going to be at school the next day. I didn't have a watch on, and I couldn't reach for my phone, but it was definitely gone midnight and Kev had already knocked the door, swearing, three times. There were times when the chef's breathing quickened a little, and I hoped he was close to finishing, but every time it happened he just took a big swig of water from his bottle and spat it on the floor, like it was some sort of weird ritual.

Around two hours had passed when Kev started knocking again. This time, he was really hammering the door and it sounded like he was going to burst in and beat the chef up.

'You bastard!' he was shouting. 'You've taken Viagra, haven't you, you fucking cunt!'

But it was well over another hour before the chef finally got bored. He hadn't finished but he climbed off me, still erect, and walked out onto the landing in his pants as I fumbled around, looking for my clothes. I could hear him telling Kev he wasn't paying because he couldn't come. Kev was going absolutely mental, telling him he was a dick for taking Viagra and he better pay up or else. I quickly shoved on my T-shirt and jeans and stood in the doorway, feeling lost.

'Just get in the car, Holly,' Kev said, 'while I deal with this dick.'

I wondered if that was the angriest I'd ever seen him and I figured it might be, which was saying something as he was a very angry man. The wind drove the rain into my face as I walked downstairs and made my way into the car.

'You were gone ages!' Carly exclaimed. I looked at the clock on the dashboard and it read 1.35 a.m. I prayed Mum and Phil were fast asleep. If for whatever reason they'd come to my room and seen that I was missing at this time, they'd go absolutely nuts.

'I'm really sore,' I said, honestly. 'He was doing it for ages. Where did you tell your mum you were going?'

Carly giggled. 'She thinks I'm at Gran's. Before you came out, Kev was getting really wound up. He said if you didn't come out soon, he'd maybe let me do it. But then you turned up so, hey. Anyway, it's fine. You always share the money with me anyway.'

With that, Kev threw open the door and plonked himself

on the driver's side. He was holding loads of cash, so I assumed the chef had paid up in full, though I'd no idea how Kev had managed to force him. Perhaps I didn't want to know.

Almost to himself, he said, 'He tried to fucking mug me off! We won't be going back to that fucking bastard again.'

A few days later at school, I was sitting in a social education class and the teacher started to talk about sexually transmitted infections. She was speaking about chlamydia. She said if you didn't catch it in time you might not be able to have kids, but in loads of cases there weren't any symptoms, so most people who had it didn't know. I felt a bit sick and Jenny leaned over to tell me I'd gone all pale. I'd seen signs about chlamydia when I'd gone to the walk-in clinic but I hadn't thought much of it, or paid much attention. I just assumed I'd know if I'd caught something like that because there would be some sort of sign. For the rest of the day, I didn't feel safe and protected like I usually did in school. I couldn't even concentrate in travel and tourism. I was just desperate to get checked out to make sure I didn't have this horrible disease festering silently inside me.

Omar hadn't mentioned sex to me. He hadn't even mentioned a blow job. But what if one day we did decide to have sex and I was riddled with this terrible infection? So far, I felt like I'd done a good job of persuading him all the rumours about me were completely made up. That's what I told myself, anyway, because surely he would have tried to get sex or a blow job if he thought I was a massive slag? Surely he wouldn't kiss me so much if he thought I'd given blow jobs to random men?

But if he caught something from me I'd have nowhere to hide, and he'd have even more reason to hate me because I'd infected him, and I'd lied.

I was so worried that I thought about palming Mr Khan off, but in the end I wasn't brave enough. Thankfully the walk-in clinic was still open when he dropped me back by the phone box. I practically ran there and asked one of the nurses if I could have a chlamydia test. She'd given me the morning-after pill loads of times, so she must have known who I was, but she pretended not to recognise me, as she handed me a form to fill in. Then she gave me a little swab and I went into the bathroom. It took two minutes but she told me the results could take up to a week to come through.

For six long days, I could barely eat or sleep. As if I didn't have enough to worry about, I was now convinced I had a disease ravaging my body. When I stole half an hour here or there with Omar, he noticed something was wrong.

'You're really quiet,' he said, nuzzling into my neck as we sat on our favourite wall, near the church but out of view of the main road. 'Everything OK?'

'Yeah, course,' I lied. 'Just tired. Nothing's wrong.'

Finally the clinic called me on my mobile and told me I was clear. I almost cried with relief. I remember thinking it was a minor miracle, as by that point I'd had unprotected sex with dozens of men and I'd convinced myself that one of them must have had it and passed it on to me. But I knew it was only a temporary reprieve. The next time one of the men paid Kev the extra twenty-five quid to shag me without a condom, I wouldn't only have to worry about going for the morning-after pill, so I wouldn't get pregnant, I'd have all of this to think of, too. Where would it end?

You might think that everything I was going through meant I didn't want to have sex with Omar, but I was so confused and mixed up that I didn't have a clue what I wanted. We'd been together nearly three months when I was at Dad's and he was heading out on a night shift. It was a Saturday, and usually my phone would be buzzing with calls from Kev, with places to go and people to see, but today he was strangely quiet.

Omar's family were really strict Muslims, so there was no way I could ever have gone round to his house, not as his girlfriend anyway, so I texted him and asked him if he wanted to come round to Dad's.

By now, Gemma and Liam were grown up and doing their own thing, so I had the place to myself. Omar and I rarely had time to ourselves, never more than half an hour, and we never got to spend any time together indoors. On that afternoon, we just sat on Dad's couch, cuddling and watching telly. It was so simple, but it felt so nice.

'Where did you tell your mum you were?' I asked him.

'Oh, just at a mate's,' he smiled, swooping in for another kiss. I draped my legs over his and we began kissing again, a bit more passionately this time. I could tell Omar was getting a bit hot and bothered but still he didn't say anything, or ask me for anything. After a few minutes, I pulled away, slowly but surely.

'My dad's on night shift,' I said, taking his hand in mine. 'He won't be back for hours.'

Omar nodded, slowly, like he wasn't really following.

I pushed a strand of hair behind my ear nervously. 'Do you want to, you know?'

He raised an eyebrow. 'You mean . . .?'

'Yes,' I said. 'Will we go into the bedroom?'

13

Betrayed

Sex with Omar was different from the sex I'd had with anyone else. Although I'd been with loads of guys before, I normally just lay there, so it wasn't like I had loads of tricks up my sleeve. It was a bit fumbling at first, but we soon got into the swing of things. We did it slowly and it wasn't rough.

I was two months shy of my fifteenth birthday and Omar was the same age. In the cold light of day, we were too young to be having sex, but sex felt like the only currency I had. Omar liked me for who I was and he'd never complained that we hadn't done anything sexual yet. But I just had this awful feeling that if I didn't do it he'd go off me. He was really good-looking and Carly said he was a bit of a heart-throb at their school, which made me feel really insecure. He'd have loads of girls after him. I had to do everything in my power to keep him, because seeing him was the only thing that made my life feel like it was worth living. If I lost him, I didn't know what I'd do.

'Do you love him?' Carly asked one evening, as we sat in the back of Beaver's car, while he delivered pizzas.

'I think I do,' I said. 'He's so fit and so lovely. He's not like Ali or any of those other lads.'

Carly shrugged. 'I don't think you do love him. If you love him, why are you still shagging other guys?'

Thankfully Beaver came back and started the car before I had time to answer. I hadn't told Beaver about Omar, as close as we were. I'm not sure why, it just felt weird, though we usually told each other everything else. I guess I figured he had enough on his plate. His wife had given birth to their baby, a little boy called Hassan, and he seemed a bit distracted. Not that he ever seemed to spend much time at home. He was always out with us, delivering his pizzas and blaring his music and doing the silly dancing, which made us laugh so much.

Omar's parents were really strict, so he was never allowed to stay out very late. I always had to see him in the early evening, usually after I'd been with Mr Khan. Our brief meetings were still the highlight of my whole day. Although we'd by now had sex, we rarely had time alone, properly alone. We could only ever do anything more than kiss when Dad was on night shift. If I took him back to Mum's, the girls would never have given him a moment's peace and, needless to say, going to his was out, so things actually still felt quite innocent in a lot of ways.

But word had begun to spread that we were together, especially around all of the lads at his school. Two of Ali's mates had caught us kissing near the church one day and then the cat was out of the bag. It became harder to ignore them. Now they had something on me, something they knew I cared about. I had something to lose and that something was Omar.

At long last, they could blackmail me.

It started one evening when I was walking to meet Omar in town. I'd just had a really nasty encounter with Mr Khan and he'd hit me hard with his iron bar. The only reason he gave was that the sex had been rubbish, but it was no different from usual. I was feeling sore and sorry for myself when an Asian lad approached me. He was a couple of years older than me and he got right up in my face. Later, much later, I'd discover that his name was Mubarek Ali.

'Hey,' he said. 'I hear you give good blow jobs. You look like you give good blow jobs. Want to give me one?'

I tried to push past him but he wouldn't let me. 'No,' I said. 'I'm going to meet my boyfriend.'

'Boyfriend?' he laughed. Suddenly I became aware of seven or eight of his mates, all crowding round me. I felt really intimidated but I tried to keep my nerve. 'Does your boyfriend know you're a little slag? Because everyone else does.'

I met his gaze and said, 'I'm not giving you a blow job.'

'Come on,' he said. 'I know you do it for everyone else. Meet me at the bowling green in ten minutes and you can sort it, yeah?'

His mates let rip a peal of laughter, as if on cue.

'No,' I said, again. I broke away from the group of lads and started to walk down the street, but Mubarek was hot on my heels. It was only after a few seconds that I realised he was chasing after me.

'Bitch,' he hissed. He'd been holding a bottle and I'd assumed it was juice but, as he threw its contents towards me, the stench of urine overpowered me. It felt warm as it collided with my face, and I winced in disgust as it ran through my hair and down my cheeks. Instinctively I went to cry out in horror, but I clamped my mouth shut so I wouldn't accidentally swallow any of it.

As I dabbed my face desperately with a tissue, hot tears of humiliation pricked my eyes. All of Mubarek's mates were hooting and howling with laughter now, as if it was the funniest thing they'd ever seen. I'd never felt shame quite like it. It was different from being hidden away in a dingy, damp room or the back seat of a car. Mubarek had made a massive public spectacle of me, and that was somehow equally awful but in a whole different way.

I knew I could never meet Omar in this state. I couldn't bring myself to explain what had happened. It was far too embarrassing. I turned to head for home, where I could clean myself up, hopefully before the next call came in from Kev.

On the way back, I got my phone out and dialled 999. I'd never thought to call the police when I'd been raped and sexually assaulted, mainly because I didn't think anyone was committing a crime. I'd agreed to go there, and I'd been paid, so I thought they'd just laugh and tell me it was my own fault.

Surely they would take this seriously, though? I hadn't asked for this and, in my opinion, it was an assault.

'I'd like to report an assault,' I said to the operator. 'Someone has just poured a bottle of pee all over me because he was asking for a blow job and I wouldn't give him one.'

The operator couldn't get me off the phone fast enough. She launched into a tirade about how I was wasting police time and that I ought to hang up and let them deal with real crimes. I felt really angry, but it just confirmed what I already suspected: no one really cared what was happening to me, because they all thought I had brought it on myself. If I thought that incident was a one-off, I was sorely mistaken, and the reaction of the police operator only made me feel more powerless.

No one else threw piss over me, but they all shouted at me that I was a slag and that they'd tell Omar. My insides would clench with dread, wondering what they would say to him and, even worse, how much of it he would believe. The irony was that most of these guys my own age didn't have a bloody clue what I got up to. They didn't know the half of it, and they'd have probably been shocked if they did. But they filled in the gaps by simply making up other things about me and by repeating the old rumour that I gave out free blow jobs to anyone who gave me the time of day.

It was a lad called Asif who made me cave first. I was on my way back from meeting Omar one time and he accosted me as I walked through the centre of town. I recognised him, as Carly had mentioned that he was in a couple of her classes and he was a bit of a dick.

'Holly,' he said, grabbing the sleeve of my denim jacket. 'Sort it for us, eh? You know you want to.'

'No,' I said. 'I've got a boyfriend. I'm not doing it.'

But Asif wasn't one for giving up. 'Omar?' he laughed. 'Yeah, whatever. Go on, just do it. I know you do it for everyone else. He'll never know.'

I was determined not to give in. Sleeping with Mr Khan and the men Kev took me to was one thing, but giving one of Omar's classmates a blow job was another. It was too close to home and, boys being boys, I just knew they'd boast about it and he'd find out in no time.

It might sound strange, but blow jobs felt different from sex.

Don't get me wrong, sex with some of the men I'd been taken to had been absolutely horrible. Most of them smelled really bad and a lot of the time it was rough, aggressive and painful. But the thought of giving someone a blow job seemed ten times worse. With blow jobs, you couldn't lie there and switch your brain down and think of other stuff. You had to be involved, to pretend you were enjoying it, to put on a big act. In most cases with Kev's men I managed to avoid it, and the only good thing about Mr Khan was that he never asked for one. I figured it was because he always wanted to kiss me.

But Asif didn't want to kiss me. I told him no again, and I tried to walk on, but he grabbed hold of my arm, his fingers digging into the sleeve of my jacket. His eyes were cold as they focused on me, and his voice dropped to a whisper.

'Do it,' he said. 'And I won't say a word to Omar.' I opened my mouth to protest, but he cut me off. 'And if you don't do it? I'll tell him you did. I'll tell him you sucked off every guy in our school.'

I closed my eyes, just for a second. I didn't say a word and, as I opened them, Asif was still standing there, smirking. I didn't even have to say yes. He knew he had me over a barrel, as he led me up an alleyway and dropped his trousers.

After Asif, I can't remember how many more blow jobs I gave out. It was always the same story. The boys would tell me that, if I didn't do it, they'd tell Omar that I had, and I couldn't cope with that. I hated every second of it, as they dragged me down alleyways or round the back of the church, and shoved my head into their crotches without a word of warning.

What made it even more repulsive was that I never did it with Omar. Not once. We had sex occasionally, when Dad was on night shift and Omar could sneak away, but most of the time we just kissed and cuddled, as we sat on some random garden wall. That's why it felt so horrible, doing it with his so-called friends.

One night, as we sat there hand in hand, Omar turned to me and said: 'I have to ask you something. There's a guy at my school called Asif.'

My heart sank, but I nodded, willing him to go on.

'Everyone says you gave him a blow job down the alleyway near the church. Is it true?'

I could feel the colour draining from my cheeks, as I dropped Omar's hand. 'If that's what you think of me, then fine,' I replied, coldly. 'If you want to believe those horrible boys over me, then go ahead. I know whose side you're on.'

Omar wrapped his arms around me. 'I'm sorry,' he said, but I pulled away.

'You think I'm a slag, don't you?' I said. 'Everyone says I am and you believe them.'

'I don't!' he cried. 'I promise! I don't think you're a slag. I'm sorry. I . . . I don't know how to say this, but I think I love you.'

My eyes widened. 'You love me?'

'Yeah,' he said. 'I do. Do you love me?'

I tried hard to swallow the lump in my throat. I was feeling so many emotions I couldn't decide which one to concentrate on. Of course there was the shame and guilt, for having done all of those things, and then lying about them, but I also felt elated that, in spite of everything everyone said about me, Omar loved me. He loved me.

'Yeah,' I said. 'I think I do.'

I suppose it's probably no surprise that after that I tried to find ways of avoiding the teenage boys who pestered me for blow jobs. The easiest way, of course, was to go off with Beaver in his car. It was much nicer, and warmer, than walking anywhere, and Beaver didn't ask anything in return. He just wanted to moan about how horrible his wife was and how hard their life was now they had a baby.

His wife had to go back to work in Tesco quite quickly after she'd given birth, so sometimes Beaver brought Hassan along when he picked up Carly and me to help him with his pizza rounds. Hassan was really cute, and I loved playing with him as he gurgled away on the back seat. I couldn't understand why Beaver thought he was such a burden, but I guessed it was probably because I didn't have a kid and I didn't get how hard it was caring for them all the time.

I really enjoyed those nights, not just because it meant I was away from all of the horrible teenage boys, but because it felt grown-up. I liked being out in a car with an older man and getting the chance to look after a baby. When I was holed up in a room with one of Kev's horrible men, or in the back of Mr Khan's car, I felt more childish than ever, but this felt good. This felt like I was a proper adult, and I didn't need to do anything sexual to prove it.

One night, I was bouncing Hassan on my knee on the back seat when I began to study the tattoo Beaver had at the top of his arm. I'd noticed it before, but I hadn't looked at it closely.

It was springtime by now, so he'd started wearing T-shirts more often. It intrigued me. I could see that it was some kind of writing, in an alphabet I didn't recognise, but I wondered what it meant. Perhaps it was the name of a girl he'd loved back home and couldn't be with, and that's why he resented his wife so much.

'Hey,' I said. 'What's the tattoo? On your arm? What does it mean?'

He didn't take his eyes off the road, as he changed gear. 'It's from when I was in prison in Pakistan.'

I could hardly believe what I was hearing. Harmless, silly Beaver in prison? He couldn't hurt a fly.

'Prison?' I laughed. 'What were you in prison for?'

Beaver wasn't smiling, though. 'Just fighting,' he replied. Then he changed the subject and started to ask me if I wanted a pizza after he'd done his next delivery. I didn't ask any more questions, but I found it all really strange. If he'd been in prison for fighting, he surely had to have really hurt someone? I could imagine Mr Khan being in prison, and even maybe Kev, but certainly not Beaver.

The only time he'd seemed really angry was when I'd told him about Mr Khan and he'd chased his car through the town, but even then they hadn't come to blows. It just didn't add up.

By the time my fifteenth birthday rolled around, I was seeing Beaver almost every night. It wasn't a conscious decision; it just seemed to happen. I hated having to walk anywhere myself because I got so much hassle and, if I was on my own, I usually had to give someone a blow job. Beaver had a car, and a car with blacked-out windows at that.

When I look back now, I'm not sure how I juggled everything. After school, I'd always see Mr Khan. Then I'd try to see Omar for half an hour before going home to do my homework. Sometimes I'd have dinner at home with my family, but other times I'd tell them I was eating with Carly and her mum, when really Kev was taking me to one of the many appointments he'd made.

He was getting bolder, and the men were getting worse. Most of them smelled awful and lots of them had no teeth. He was telling me to meet him in the middle of the night more often, so I'd have to sneak in and out of the house and then get up for school the next day like I'd had a full night's sleep. Astonishingly Mum and Phil never seemed to realise I'd been gone. There were times I ached for them to notice, as much as I knew I'd be in big trouble from Kev if I didn't turn up. Didn't they see the pain on my face, the bags under my eyes? For a long time, I would resent them for this. But I guess I can't really blame them, because, by this point, I was really good at sneaking around.

Nearly all the men I was taken to were Asian immigrants of some kind, or at least the sons of Asian immigrants. In the whole time Kev was exploiting and selling me, I only remember being sent to one white British man. I think he was from Scotland. He wanted a blow job and he was just as disgusting as all of the rest. A lot has been made of this in recent years, but back then it didn't matter to me what colour skin a man had or what language he spoke. As he lay his disgusting body on top of me and did what he'd paid to do, he could have been bloody purple for all I cared. I just wanted it to be over.

I did wonder if Omar had started to doubt me when I insisted all of the rumours were complete lies. Sometimes he'd look like he wanted to ask me something, but then he'd stop and change the subject. It was my word against everyone else's, and I knew he stuck up for me.

Perhaps stupidly, I started to buy him things with the money I'd made from Kev. I had loads in my little stash now, but I still didn't want to look at it or acknowledge it was there. I couldn't get rid of it fast enough and, if Omar said he liked something, even in passing, I'd go out and buy it straight away.

'Wow, Holly,' he said, as I handed him yet another new shirt. 'Thanks so much. But how have you managed to pay for this?'

'Oh, my dad gives me money every week because he doesn't live with us,' I replied, breezily.

It was kind of true, but he didn't give us half as much as I was making from Kev, and it would never have stretched to cover all the things I bought for Omar. I've wrestled with myself since, wondering if Omar was taking advantage, but I really don't think he was. He never asked for anything, really, and it was always me who was more than eager to buy him stuff and get rid of the money that made me feel horrible and dirty.

Things all came to a head about six months into our relationship, though. I'd started taking Omar to Mum's, usually when she wasn't in, but occasionally she'd come home from work to find us sitting on the sofa watching telly, that's if I didn't have an arrangement with Kev. Omar never stayed long because his parents always wanted him back for dinner.

At first, Mum didn't seem to mind, because Omar was polite and didn't cause any trouble. But one Saturday afternoon he'd come round for an hour when I started to quiz him on what he'd like from the shops.

'I've got extra money from my dad this week,' I lied. 'So pick anything you like and I'll give you the money.'

In the end, Omar decided he wanted some new Rockport boots and, as he went to leave to walk home, I handed him sixty quid. I didn't realise Mum was watching from the window and she came tearing out of the house like a woman possessed.

'Are you giving that boy money?' she cried. 'The money your dad gives you?'

I froze. I hadn't given Omar the money Dad had given me, but I wasn't really supposed to have any other money. There was no way of explaining this to Mum, unless I told her the truth, which was unthinkable. I didn't say anything, but I didn't have to. Mum was running up the street, looking for Omar, but he'd already disappeared round the corner.

'Do you think we've got the money for you to waste on some boy?' she said, as she swung open the gate and pushed her way back into the garden. 'Do you think money grows on trees?'

I shook my head, sullenly.

'This isn't the last of this,' she said, breathless from trying to run after Omar. 'I'll be phoning your dad and he'll be speaking to that lad. That money is for clothes and school books and things you need. Not to just give away to some random boy. You're not to see him again. Do you understand?'

I rolled my eyes, like most teenagers would have done, and said nothing, but I almost wanted to laugh. Mum banning me from seeing Omar seemed almost laughable. If only she knew all of the other things that were going on in my life, me giving money to a boy so he could buy a pair of boots would be the least of her worries.

It made things a bit awkward, though. Dad did speak to Omar and he gave me the money back. I didn't want the money, and I didn't want Omar to feel awkward, so it made me upset. Mum and Dad both seemed to have it in for Omar big time from then on, and Mum made it clear he wasn't welcome in the house, so we were back to meeting in town and kissing and cuddling for twenty minutes on a garden wall before I disappeared back to my other life – a life no teenager should have.

The only other person I felt like I could talk to about my weird home life was Beaver. Sometimes I don't think he understood quite what I said when I ranted about Mum, but at least he listened and didn't tell me to shut up. I tried not to call him Beaver to his face, but sometimes it slipped out.

'Why you call me this, Beaver?' he'd ask, bemused, but he never seemed to object much, even when I showed him a picture on my phone of an actual beaver to try to help him learn the English word. I just really don't think he got it, to be honest.

One night I was out really late with him. It was a Friday and I didn't have school the next day, so Mum didn't mind if I stayed at Carly's a little longer than usual. Of course, I was rarely actually at Carly's, but it was my go-to excuse. We were driving through town, just the two of us. His wife wasn't working, so Hassan was at home with her, and Carly was visiting family up north somewhere with her gran.

We were on a street in Wellington, with all of the pizzas in the back, near the church where we'd first met, when I became aware of flashing blue lights in the rear-view mirror. It took me several seconds to realise it was a police car, because the sirens weren't on. But the lights kept shining into the car and along the dashboard and I quickly figured they wanted Beaver to pull over.

'You need to stop,' I said. 'It's the police.'

He pulled into a lay-by and the police stopped behind him, telling him to get out. As he opened the door, one of the officers looked straight at me but he didn't say a word. Then, he and his colleague searched the boot of the car and asked Beaver a few questions, like his name and address. He didn't tell the truth about who he was, which I thought was a bit strange, but I couldn't hear the conversation properly. No one asked who I was. Maybe the police assumed I was over sixteen, but I doubt it. Back then, I was quite glad they didn't probe too much, as I thought they might take me home to Mum in a police car, and then I'd have a lot of explaining to do about why I wasn't at Carly's. Now, though, I think quite differently.

'What was that all about?' I asked Beaver.

'Nothing,' he laughed. 'Stupid bastards.'

He dropped me home like nothing had happened, so I assumed it was no big deal.

It was a few nights later when things changed forever. We were out delivering pizzas alone again when Beaver unexpectedly pulled into the side of the road. It was really dark and quiet and there was no one around, but I didn't feel scared, just a bit confused.

'What are you doing?' I asked, with a little laugh. 'Why have you stopped?'

Beaver had turned off the ignition and all the dashboard lights had gone out. I could see the moonlight shining on his face, his yellowing teeth protruding in the darkness. It took me a few seconds to realise he was fiddling with the zip on his trousers, and at first I thought he was going out for a pee at the side of the road.

'Holly,' he said. 'I want you to suck my dick.'

14

Who Can I Trust?

I sank back in my seat, in shock. What I'd heard Beaver say just didn't compute, and for a few moments I was completely dumbstruck. It sounds naive, but I'd almost totally forgotten that he'd showed me his dick once before, the time we'd first met. The Beaver who took me on his pizza deliveries, and did his silly dancing, and let me play with his son, seemed like a completely different person to the one who'd exposed himself to me at the foot of the Wrekin – the one who looked lost and couldn't speak a word of English.

'No!' I eventually managed to splutter. 'No! We're mates. I'm not doing that with you, no!'

I expected Beaver to give me one of his bashful, toothy grins and a little shrug. He'd tried his luck, I'd said no, and that was that. But, as I looked at his face in the darkness, I could see something in his eyes which scared me. Something different, something that had never been there before. His chest rose and fell a few times, as he stared at me, breathing deeply.

But his voice was soft when he spoke, almost a whisper.

'Go on,' he said. 'You are my *jaan*. My love.' He reached over to take my hand, but I snatched it away. 'I love you.'

I was horrified. 'Bloody hell!' I exclaimed. 'You have a wife! Jeez, you don't love me, we're just mates!'

He looked crestfallen, as he turned the key back in the ignition and the dashboard lit up again. It sounds crazy, but I felt sorry for him. I didn't see him as a thirty-year-old man preying on a vulnerable, abused fifteen-year-old. I didn't grasp that our relationship could never be equal, that he had always had the power and always would. I just felt a bit mean because I hadn't let him down gently.

'My wife doesn't understand me like you do, Holly,' he said, still quietly, as the engine roared into life and he pulled back onto the road. I folded my hands in my lap and stared at the ground, feeling awkward. There were just two more pizzas in the back of the car and, for once, I was glad it was almost time to go home.

It took me a few minutes to realise that Beaver was heading out of Telford. He started driving really fast, the way he had done the day we'd chased Mr Khan. He took a corner with such speed that I had to hold on to the door handle, knuckles white. Neither of us said a single word as we hurtled along the country roads, the Wrekin slowly getting closer and closer, casting its ever-growing shadow over the town.

Beaver swung into the deserted car park and pulled on the handbrake with such force I went flying forward and almost hit my head on the glove compartment. If I'd thought the Wrekin looked scary at sunset, it was positively terrifying now. The clock on the dashboard said it was gone eleven – the latest I'd ever been here.

The only sound was the faint hooting of a single owl,

somewhere in the distance. Out of the window, the sky was so clear I could see the stars strewn across the deep, midnight-blue sky. If I'd been somewhere else, I might have thought it looked really pretty, but now it felt menacing and scary.

And even though I was sitting right next to Beaver – the guy I'd come to think of as a mate, maybe even my best mate – I felt like I was alone.

Really, really alone.

It was so dark I could hardly see a thing, just the outline of some trees fluttering softly in the gentle night breeze. Slowly, Beaver moved his hand from the gearstick to my knee and my whole leg tensed up. We just stared at each other for a few seconds, frozen in a strange kind of deadlock.

Finally, I broke the silence. 'What are we doing here?' I asked. 'You're not going to deliver a pizza here, are you?'

I sounded braver than I felt. Beaver let out a knowing laugh and he stroked the inside of my thigh with his fingers, over my jeans. His touch made me squirm and he was so close I could smell the stale fags on his breath.

'You are my *jaan*,' he said. 'You are my love. Go on, please. Please. I love you.'

Nausea gripped me and I had to wait a second for it to pass. I'd never felt so betrayed in all my life. Since this whole thing began, I'd been tricked by lots of people: Ali, Imran, Mr Khan, Kev, Asif – the list was endless. But this was the one betrayal that hurt the most. It hurt because I thought Beaver was my mate. I thought he wanted to protect me. I didn't want to believe he was just like the rest of them, I just couldn't.

'No,' I said, as gently as I could, trying to change tack in the hope it would make him see sense. 'No, let's not. It will ruin things. I don't think we should.'

Beaver — sweet, bashful, silly Beaver — brought his hand down on the steering wheel with a huge thud. It made me jump but, as he turned to face me, there was rage in his eyes. Pure rage. I recognised that rage so well — the rage that all these older men felt when they didn't get their own way. From Mr Khan, when I wouldn't kiss him, to Kev, when I was ten minutes late for an appointment.

But I never thought I'd see that rage in Beaver's eyes.

'You're a fucking bitch if you don't do it,' he spat. 'You do it with everyone else.'

Quietly, I said, 'I don't want to.'

Beaver turned away from me and looked into the distance, the vast expanse of countryside that stretched for miles around, all covered by this thick sheet of darkness. The little owl hooted again before he spoke.

'Fine,' he said. 'But if you don't do it, you have to get out.'

I could feel the tears springing to my eyes, but I took a deep breath and turned away for a second to compose myself, otherwise they'd have spilled all down my cheeks and I would have looked like a total baby. I bit my lip really hard and the taste of warm blood filled my mouth.

As I gazed out of the window on the passenger side, the lump in my throat slowly subsided and gave way to anger. I hated the Wrekin now. I bloody hated it. I couldn't understand how I could have ever been happy there as a child because now, every time it slid into view, looming over the town as if it was watching everyone and everything, I got a knot of dread in my stomach. Tonight, it looked like a scene from the start of a horror film, where everything is eerily dark and silent but you know something really, really bad is going to happen, where you're just waiting for the bad guy to jump out of the bushes, grab a young girl and do something terrible. I had two choices: give Beaver a blow job, or have him leave me here all alone.

It wasn't really a choice, was it?

As we got into the back seat and he dropped his trousers, confusion tore my brain apart. Beaver had been so angry at Mr Khan whenever he dumped me in the middle of nowhere. He'd torn after him in his car the day he beat me with the belt and abandoned me; he'd almost run Mr Khan off the road. Since then, it had happened countless times, but Beaver always came and collected me. He always picked up the pieces. Now he was threatening to do exactly the same thing.

How could he be the same as them? How could he?

Yet, as he dropped his jeans and pulled down his pants, I thought to myself: I don't want to lose him. I didn't have many friends, really, when you thought about it. There was Carly, of course, and Jenny, and the girls from school, but because I never saw them outside of class I didn't feel like a proper part of the group and I could never, ever have told them what I was doing when I turned down invitations to shopping trips and sleepovers. Beaver knew me better than most people my own age and I couldn't imagine what it would be like if we fell out.

When he reached out and touched my head, I thought he was going to shove it straight into his crotch. But he started playing with a strand of my hair, twisting it round his finger, saying things in Urdu that I didn't understand. As his hand moved across to stroke my cheek, I caught sight of his prison tattoo, that strange collection of letters from the faraway place he'd come from, so alien to a teenager in a town in the West Midlands. As he continued to palm at my face with his rough, chubby fingers, it hit me that the prison tattoo was all I knew of his past life in Pakistan. He never spoke of his family, or the village where he'd grown up.

So all I knew was that he'd hurt someone. He'd really, really hurt someone.

I could still smell the fags on his breath, as he leaned forward to kiss me with those big, horrible, goofy teeth. I felt completely repulsed, not just because he smelled and looked weird, but because kissing him just felt so wrong. I thought of him as being a bit like a daft older brother. Snogging him just didn't compute. I turned, so his wet mouth collided with the side of my face, his big teeth brushing my cheekbone. I just wanted to get things over with, so I knelt down in front of him, and did what I had to do.

After the night at the Wrekin, things with Beaver were never the same. For a start, I decided I was now going to call him Beaver to his face. We'd barely turned out of the car park at the Wrekin when I told him he was a beaver bastard and that's what I'd be calling him from now on. He didn't say anything. I'm still not sure he understood that I was trying to insult him. He just seemed happy he'd got a blow job, so I guess he wasn't bothered what I called him.

'OK, Holly,' he said, grinning that horrible grin with his discoloured teeth, 'my *jaan*.'

Yet I still continued to go out with him on his deliveries. You might wonder why, when he'd betrayed me in such an awful, callous way. But by then my way of thinking was so twisted that I convinced myself it was somehow my fault. I told myself that maybe, just maybe, he was right. Maybe it wasn't fair that all these other men got what they wanted from me but he didn't. After all, he was the one who was nice to me, wasn't he? And he was an adult, while I was still a child. What if he really did know better?

I guess I thought he was the lesser of many evils. He didn't beat me like Mr Khan, or farm me out to disgusting men like Kev, or threaten to tell Omar like all of the teenage boys who demanded blow jobs. The only difference was that I was now more anxious for Carly to come along any time we met up.

Beaver didn't seem to mind, and it was a few weeks before the subject of blow jobs came up again. Every time he picked me up, I waited for him to bring it up, to threaten to dump me if I didn't do it, but he carried on delivering his pizzas and dancing to his Pakistani music just like before.

'What toppings would you like tonight, Holly?' he'd ask, as he parked up in the takeaway car park like nothing had happened. I even began to hope the whole sordid episode at the Wrekin was a one-off, but bitter experience should have taught me better, because then something happened that made me feel really strange.

Beaver got Carly involved.

I stupidly thought having Carly in the car might mean he didn't do anything. When we'd sat in the back seat at the foot of the Wrekin, I got the sense that he wanted it to be our dirty little secret, though he never said so out loud. Plus – this sounds so mean, and even now I feel terrible writing it – I didn't really think he'd want Carly to do anything with him because she was so fat. She practically begged Kev to sell her because she wanted to make some easy money, and even he was never keen.

So, I didn't really know how to feel as he parked up at the foot of the Wrekin one afternoon a few weeks later, and turned not to me but to Carly.

'I want a blow job,' he announced. 'But you're not going to do it. She's going to do it.'

I looked at Carly, unsure what to do or say, but she didn't seem at all bothered. Maybe she thought Beaver would give her money, like all the men who paid me, but I knew he was too skint and cheap to do that. She was already scrambling out of the back seat, while Beaver told me I could go for a walk round the car park until they were finished.

'Don't go far,' he warned me – not that I was likely to disappear on my own.

He and Carly headed off to some nearby bushes and I just sat in the front seat, sulking. I wasn't sure what or who I was mad at, but that had become my life. I was always angry at so many people and so many situations that I often forgot what was pissing me off at that particular moment in time. I'll admit I did feel a little guilty that Carly was having to give Beaver a blow job, but I pushed the thought to the back of my mind and told myself she was up for it, far more up for it than I was. For once, I was feeling something I didn't get to feel very often, and that was the tiniest hint of relief. I knew it wouldn't last long, but for five short minutes I couldn't silence a little voice in my head. The voice that said: Thank God, for once, it's not me.

It wasn't me having to smell the minging fag breath of an older man, or hold my breath as he came at me with his horrible, furry teeth, ready to stick his tongue down my throat. Someone else would have to sit there as a sweaty man writhed around all over her and made her do what no teenage girl should be doing to anyone, let alone someone twice her age.

It just so happened that someone was my best friend. But what could I do?

They weren't gone long. When they came back to the car, Carly's high ponytail was all askew, and she had some stray leaves and twigs in her hair. As she climbed into the back seat, Beaver didn't look smug, like I'd expected him to, but really annoyed.

'She's a fat bitch,' he spat, as he pulled the handbrake off and sped out of the car park. 'It was shit.'

He didn't attempt to lower his voice and Carly heard every word. I looked at her to see how she'd react but she was picking a twig from her hair and fixing her ponytail like nothing had happened.

'Oh fuck off, you dickhead,' she replied, eventually. 'You're a smelly fucking bastard.'

In the space of a year or so, both Carly and I had changed massively. The naive little girl who wore her hair in plaits and spent most of her time hanging around with her gran was long gone. Now Carly was mouthy, swore all the time and thought nothing of giving a blow job to a man twice her age. She might not have had to sleep with all the men that I had, but she was being abused and exploited, too. Her weight was constantly used as a weapon against her, and her only defence was to pretend she didn't give a shit, and that she was up for everything she did because she thought it was a laugh. Maybe she'd got to the stage where she did think it was a laugh. We were both so brainwashed it was entirely possible.

'You're going to have to get out,' Beaver told her. 'You're a fucking bitch.'

We were in the middle of a country road on the way back into town and my stomach turned over as I realised he might dump us there. I remember feeling grateful that at least it was light and we wouldn't have to walk home in the dark.

'Oh, fuck off,' said Carly. 'Do what you want.' I turned round and shot her a look, as if to tell her to pipe down, but she didn't take any notice. 'Beaver fucking bastard.'

Beaver's face contorted with anger as he drove along the stony path, and I wondered if he was slowing to a halt. But he kept driving back towards Telford, occasionally glancing in the rear-view mirror to glower at Carly. Eventually he parked up outside her gran's house and told me to let her out of the back seat.

'Why should I move?' I asked him. 'If you want her out, you move.'

He got out of the driver's seat and pulled it forward by the lever. 'Out, you fucking bitch,' he said.

Carly clambered onto the pavement. It was only then that I noticed she still had an imprint of dirt and leaves all up the back of her huge white T-shirt.

'Well, you coming Holly?' she asked. 'You're not staying with this prick, are you?'

I didn't know what to do. I felt bad for Carly, of course I did. Beaver had made her give him a blow job and then he'd had the cheek to call her a fat bitch and practically thrown her out of his car. But she had kind of been up for it, and at least it was the middle of the afternoon and he hadn't dumped her like Mr Khan often dumped me. If I got out now, Carly would want to walk into town and then we'd just get hassle from all the teenage boys who taunted us. I didn't say anything, as I sat back in the passenger seat, my seatbelt still fastened. I just gave a little shrug.

'You're a fucking bitch,' Carly said, slamming the door and running off into the house, twigs still falling from her hair.

Carly was mad at me for a few days and, without her, I didn't really have anything to do except hang around with Beaver and wait for calls from Kev. I felt bad, of course, but I didn't really have the energy to mull over our little falling-out. To me, it just didn't seem like a big deal. Deep down, I knew what Beaver had done to her was wrong, very wrong. But in my warped little world it somehow didn't seem that bad. It could have been ten times worse. She could have been beaten to a pulp; it could have been dark; she could have been alone. I just left her to stew, knowing she'd eventually get back in touch.

Plus, there was still Omar. I was over the moon when my phone lit up with a text from him later that evening. I'd now taken to meeting him in out-of-the-way side streets, away from the main roads, as there was less chance of any of his mates seeing me and shouting abuse.

As he wrapped me into a hug, I felt safe and warm for a few seconds, and I wished I could stand on the pavement in his arms forever. But as I moved to kiss him, he pulled away. He looked faintly disgusted, a bit like I probably looked when Beaver or Mr Khan tried to snog me.

All of a sudden, I felt panicky. Didn't he find me attractive anymore?

'What's wrong?' I asked, bemused.

'I love you, Holly,' Omar began. 'And I want to kiss you. I just don't know whose dick you've had in your mouth.'

15

Two Blue Lines

I felt lost now that Omar didn't want to kiss me. I knew he'd started to believe the rumours about me and I guess I couldn't really blame him. It was my word against that of pretty much every other teenage boy from his community. It was a strange situation, though, because he didn't want to break up with me. We still met up every day, we still cuddled and we even occasionally had sex, but only when Dad was on night shift because Mum still refused to have him in the house. We just never kissed anymore.

A few days after the Beaver incident, Carly and I made up, just as I'd predicted. I think I offered to buy her some make-up from town and that won her round. We didn't talk much about it, really. It was strange, but after a few weeks it was like the thing with Carly had never happened. She started coming out in the car with us again, and the incident was never mentioned by either of them. But Beaver didn't ask Carly for another blow job. His focus had shifted back to me.

One evening, we'd just dropped her home when Beaver said he needed to go to Tesco for bread and milk. We parked up but I knew not to get out of the car because his wife worked in there. It did occur to me that she could have come out at any moment and seen me sitting in the front seat, but I just told myself I'd deal with that situation if it arose.

'My wife is being a fucking bitch,' said Beaver. 'Always shouting at me because Hassan is naughty.'

He went into the shop and he was back within minutes, tossing his carrier bag onto the back seat. 'She is so mad, today. Bitch.'

Although Beaver was saying such horrible things about his wife, I still felt a bit sorry for him when he moaned about his home life. It was like my brain was programmed to feel pity for him, no matter how much I tried to fight it. At the time, I really believed his wife was a bitch, though now I know she probably wasn't.

I could tell we were heading for the Wrekin again. I didn't even have to ask. As he drove there, Beaver was still moaning about how he had no money and how he didn't want to go home because things were so hard.

'Being with you, Holly,' he said. 'That is when I'm happy. That's the only time I'm happy.'

I didn't say anything. I just leaned forward and turned up the volume on the stereo so Beaver's music reverberated around the car and the sounds from a country far away filled my ears. The music was OK, I guess. It wasn't really my cup of tea – I was still obsessed with Ja Rule – but it wasn't the worst and it was far better than listening to Beaver tell me he loved me.

We parked up and, as usual, there were no other cars around. It was deathly silent. I couldn't even hear the little owl hooting softly in the distance. I looked to the sky, but it wasn't clear that night. I could hardly see any stars and misty grey clouds floated around the almost full moon.

'Give me a cuddle,' Beaver said. 'I need a cuddle. Let's get in the back.'

Without even thinking, I climbed over the gearstick and onto the back seat. Beaver did the same and sat down next to me, resting his hand on my leg. We just sat there in silence for a few seconds before he started singing me a song in Urdu, his voice soft and the moonlight streaking his face.

'What the hell are you singing?' I asked.

'A love song,' he said. 'A love song for you, from my country. Because you are my *jaan*, my darling.'

I didn't reply. I just turned and looked out of the window, as he started playing with my hair again, brushing his lips against my cheeks. With a little more force, he pulled my face, so I was looking straight into his eyes. His fag breath nearly knocked me out as I struggled a little, to break free, but he forced his lips on me and tried to stick his tongue down my throat. As I clasped my mouth shut, his huge, protruding teeth collided with my top lip.

That didn't put him off. He started to reach for the button at the top of my jeans and I batted his hand away.

'Come on, darling,' he said. 'I always look after you. I protect you, I love you. Please?'

I shook my head. 'No.'

'Please?' he said again, like he hadn't heard. 'For me, my *jaan*?' He didn't wait for an answer. Now he was pawing at my breasts, tugging at my T-shirt. Before long, I was in my underwear, clothes in a little pile beneath me on the upholstery. The tears came slowly but surely, stinging my eyes as they spilled down my cheeks and onto my naked breasts, as Beaver had unhooked my bra.

'What's wrong, darling?' he asked, stroking my wet cheek like he didn't know.

'We're supposed to be friends,' I said, hoarsely.

Beaver smiled, revealing all of his horrible, neglected teeth. 'Holly, my *jaan*. You *are* my best friend.'

The sex was more aggressive than I expected it to be. I certainly didn't feel like one of the girls in Beaver's Urdu love songs. When it was over, I pulled on my clothes in a trance and got back into the front of the car. I turned off his Pakistani music and flicked the radio to a local station, which was playing R&B. I turned the volume up so loud the car started to shake. As we turned back towards Telford, I looked at my phone to find three missed calls and a text from Kev.

Got someone coming down from Birmingham. He wants a girl. Meet me at 9 p.m. End of road. Don't be late!!!

It was already a quarter to, so I told Beaver to drive me home because Mum was moaning at me for staying out late. He did as I said without much protest. He'd already got what he wanted from me, at least for one night.

As I climbed out of Beaver's car and walked down the street to where Kev was waiting, two police officers walked past. One of them looked from me towards Beaver's car, which had already started to speed away. He looked like he might say something, like he might ask me who I'd been with and what we'd been doing. But he obviously changed his mind because he walked on without a word.

'Where have you been?' Kev barked, as he threw open the door. 'We're going to be late.'

I mumbled some explanation about how I'd been at Carly's but he wasn't even listening, so I just looked out of the window as we drove towards a grey industrial estate on the outside of the town. We drove out to where the services are, at the M54 junction, to the car park of a big budget hotel. It was a Friday night. I should have been out having fun with friends my own age, going to the cinema or maybe even trying my luck and attempting to get into one of the local pubs.

But no. Here I was, being driven out to a two-star hotel to meet a man who would pay me for sex. Would he be the four-teenth man I'd slept with this week, or the fifteenth? I'd lost track. I'd also lost track of when I'd last taken the morning-after pill. It had either been Tuesday or Wednesday, but I wasn't sure. I hoped it was Tuesday because then it wouldn't look quite so awful if I went back for it on Saturday morning. Or at least in my messed-up brain, that's what I thought.

We waited in the car park for about five minutes, before Kev's phone started to ring. Walking towards the car was a morbidly obese Pakistani man. He was easily the fattest person I'd ever seen in the flesh, like the kind you see in crazy American documentaries about people who eat ten Big Macs a day. I figured he was easily thirty stone, if not heavier. He was wearing a grey suit that was around five sizes too small for him. He looked like he was about to burst out of it. His fat creased in five or six huge rolls around his stomach and it was hard to tell where his chin stopped and his neck began. As he edged closer, I could see he'd dropped food all down the white string vest he wore underneath his suit jacket.

I'd got really good at switching off and closing down my senses when these nameless men were presented to me, so I didn't have to feel them or smell them or look at them. But, once in a while, a man would come along who was just so repulsive that it was hard to do anything but gag. This was one of those times.

Kev saw the horror written all over my face, but he didn't care. All he wanted was this man's money.

'The sooner you do it, the sooner it's over,' he said. 'Off you go.'

The man led me through the reception and up to one of the cramped little rooms. We had to go in the lift because he couldn't manage the stairs, but the whole way up to the second floor I wondered if his huge bulk might cause it to crash. To my horror, he started to make small talk with me, asking me if I liked Telford, and wasn't this a nice hotel? I longed to tell him I hated Telford, it was a shithole, and so was this fucking god-awful hotel. But I just made do with monosyllabic grunts.

The fat man turned the key in the lock and flicked on the dim light. The room was basic, as I'd expected, but I consoled myself with the fact that it was at least cleaner than the upstairs of a takeaway, with its smell of stale curry, or the damp back bedroom in Kev's second house. There was a double bed, with cheap-looking white sheets, and a table with a little lamp. In the corner of the room there was a door, which I assumed led to a bathroom but I didn't venture to find out. I just wanted to get in and out as soon as I could.

'Let me just go and wash my armpits,' the man said, and I winced in horror as he popped into the bathroom and ran the tap for a few seconds.

He obviously hadn't used any soap because he smelled really bad as he took off his dirty suit and rolled onto the bed, already breathless with the effort. The stench of old sweat was overpowering. I tried so hard to zone out but this time it just wasn't possible. I lay down next to him and he tried to roll on top of me, but I couldn't bear his weight. It just didn't work, because he was so huge.

We tried a couple of different positions but the only thing that worked was me climbing on top of him. I'd never done that before, and I hated every second, but I had to do all the work, to really feel involved. Thankfully he didn't take too long. As soon as I was finished I grabbed my clothes and got out as fast as I could, leaving him festering and wheezing in sick satisfaction on the hard bed.

As I climbed back into the car, Kev seemed to think it was all a huge laugh.

'Ha!' he said. 'What a fucking fat bastard! Sad prick.'

I could still smell the man's sweat on me as I got out of the car. Kev didn't give me any money, not a single penny. Not even twenty-five quid for the morning-after pill.

I went to the clinic the next morning and paid for the pill from my own stash of notes. Again, there was a flash of recognition on the nurse's face. After all, I'd only been there a few days earlier. I didn't realise it was bad for you to keep taking the pill over and over again. I took it almost every week, sometimes twice. But no one in that clinic said a single word to me. No one pulled me to one side and asked if I was OK, did I need any advice about anything? No one suggested I get the implant, or go on the pill, or even sent me away with a big stash of condoms. They just took my money and gave me the tablets like they'd never seen me before in their lives.

A few weeks later, I was feeling tired and sluggish. I'd gone out in the car with Beaver but I'd swapped my leggings for jogging bottoms because they felt so tight. He drew up outside the pizza shop and I expected him to go in and get me a margherita with extra cheese. I hoped he would, because I was bloody starving.

Instead, he lowered his voice and said: 'There are two guys who live up there – my friends. If you have sex with them, they'll give you twenty pounds.'

I thought nothing could shock me anymore, but I was wrong. Beaver didn't just want to have sex with me himself; he wanted to sell me to his mates. I threw open the door and jumped out in disgust. This time I was so angry I didn't care about being alone in the dark.

'How dare you?' I said. 'Is that all you think I'm worth, twenty quid?'

Beaver's face fell. 'You do it for Kev. Everyone knows you do.'

I couldn't deny it but I was still fuming, so I slammed the door and started to walk. Beaver crawled along beside me for a mile and a half, grovelling and telling me he was so sorry, he didn't mean to upset me, he was a stupid man, he thought I liked that kind of thing. Eventually I got tired of walking. I was always tired now, but I lived a pretty exhausting life. I climbed back into the car but I folded my arms and turned away to indicate to Beaver that I was still in a mood with him, and that I didn't want to talk.

'Why don't we go and get Carly?' he grinned, flashing his big teeth. 'She'll definitely do it.'

I'd just turned sixteen when we were given study leave from school, to prepare for our GCSEs. I hadn't really done any revision, because I didn't have a spare minute, but somehow I was still on course to pass everything, possibly because I never wanted to miss a day of school. My travel and tourism teacher told me I might even get an A because I'd done really well in my mock exam. School was still my safe haven, although I was slowly drifting apart from Jenny and the other girls. We didn't fall out or anything, and they were still really nice to me when we were in class together. I just found it difficult to join in their conversations because I never hung around with them at the weekends and I didn't really know what it was like to be a normal teenager and to do normal teenage things. I think they assumed I was just so caught up with having a boyfriend that I didn't have time for my friends.

I guess, also, I found their conversations a bit boring. They always talked about kissing boys like it was some massive deal and they shrieked with excitement when Jayne started talking about some guy in the year above who'd touched her boobs while they were snogging. While they were all squealing and giggling, I was staring out of the window of the school canteen. I must have looked a bit bored.

'How far have you gone with Omar?' Jenny asked. Her voice dropped to a whisper. 'Have you shagged him?'

Thankfully the bell rang, so we didn't have to talk any more about it. I found my school friends' innocence a little irritating. They all thought I was really grown-up and a bit of a rebel because I had a boyfriend from another school who they'd heard looked like Peter Andre.

'You are *so* lucky,' Jayne sighed, and I wanted to weep.

My next class was travel and tourism and I was really glad, as it meant a bit of an escape from the real world – or so I thought. I had just opened my books and taken out my pen when Jamal, one of the two Asian boys in the class, leaned forward and tapped me on the shoulder.

'Psst, Holly,' he said. 'I saw you the other night.'

I froze in horror.

Without daring to turn round, I said, 'Couldn't have been me, must have been someone else.'

'No, I did,' he insisted. 'You were getting into a car with this guy I know. His wife is my friend's cousin.'

Jenny dropped her pen and looked from Jamal to me to Jamal again. 'Oh my God, can Omar drive?'

The teacher was still writing something on the board with her scratchy white chalk. I longed for her to turn round and tell us all to shut up, to remind us how close our exams were, but she didn't flinch.

'No, not Omar,' Jamal said. 'This guy. I don't know his name but he looks a bit like a rat or something.'

I shook my head vigorously and forced out a laugh. 'What are you on about? What would I be doing getting into a car with a married man, you dickhead? It must have been someone else.'

As much as I liked Jamal, I felt weird being in the same class as him now. He knew too much, and I was actually glad when we had our last lesson, but I was caught between a rock and a hard place, as I was kind of dreading study leave. I'd be in the house alone all day while Mum and Phil were at work and the girls at school and nursery. Liam had gone off to university by now and Gemma had a flat of her own in the centre of town. I hoped that Kev and Mr Khan and the others didn't find out I was home alone all day or my phone would never stop ringing.

Only a few weeks had passed since Beaver had first had sex with me, but he had now started to take me to this horrible dosshouse a few streets away from Kev's houses. It belonged to an old Pakistani man who was disabled and couldn't speak much English, so Beaver would get me to fill in his forms so he could get his benefits.

It was full of really, *really* dodgy characters – one tried to get me to give him my bank details, so he could use me as part of some big fraud. He promised me £2,000 if I'd let him transfer loads of money into my account temporarily, but I didn't want any money. I was just scared of what would happen if I said no. Beaver got involved and told me not to do it or I'd go to prison, and then he and the man had a really ridiculous fight. It looked like the scene in *Bridget Jones's Diary* when Colin Firth and Hugh Grant are scrapping in the restaurant, except the characters were a lot seedier. It made me feel really confused again. If Beaver wasn't my mate, why was he standing up for me like that? I didn't know what to think.

Needless to say, the house was totally disgusting. The walls were stained yellow with nicotine because everyone just sat there and smoked all day long.

'Would you like a cup of tea?' Beaver asked one day, as I was trying to help translate a letter the old man had received about his disability allowance.

I visibly grimaced. The idea of eating or drinking anything in that house made me feel physically sick. None of the men looked like they'd washed a dish or bought a bottle of washing-up liquid in their life.

'No, thanks,' I replied. 'Why do I have to keep looking at these forms? Can't someone else do it? I'm not his secretary.'

Beaver sighed. 'Oh, please, Holly, don't be like that. If you don't do it, his money might get stopped. And then he'll have nothing. You wouldn't want him to starve, would you?'

I exhaled slowly. 'I guess not.'

Sometimes when we went to the house Beaver would take me upstairs and we'd have sex in a really minging, mouldy room on top of a bare, moth-eaten mattress. It was always quite quick. Sometimes he did it with a fag in his mouth and the ash wouldn't even have dropped off by the time he'd finished.

Looking back, it's sometimes hard to comprehend exactly how much can happen in the space of just a few weeks. It was during study leave that I became friends with a girl called Natalie. She was two years older than me and had a Pakistani boyfriend – one of the men who sometimes hung around in the

old man's house. Her boyfriend – well, at least she called him
her boyfriend – was well over forty and really, really scary.
He'd never said much to me. He just had this look about him
which told you not to mess with him. Everyone called him
Andy, but of course that wasn't his real name; a bit like Kev
wasn't really called Kev. Andy's son was friends with Omar,
and that made me really wary of him. I just tried to keep out
of his way.

Natalie was brash and loud and said what she was thinking
all the time. She was a bit like Carly in that respect, except
much, much cooler. When she swore, she didn't sound like
an idiot. She had bleached blonde hair and huge gold hooped
earrings. She was always smoking.

'I love being fucked up the arse by Andy,' she said, blowing
smoke into the air, as we stood outside the dosshouse one night.
'Have you ever been fucked up the arse?'

Natalie was only eighteen but she seemed much more experienced than even I was. Plus, she insisted to anyone who'd listen
that she loved every minute of it. If you listened to her for long
enough, she'd have you believe that shagging loads of middle-
aged men was the best fun a teenage girl could possibly have.

'I love shagging Pakis,' she went on, as she stubbed her
fag out on the wall. 'They're great in bed. Got bigger dicks,
too. Hey, you should come out with me for a drink sometime.
Would be fun.'

With that, she disappeared. As I stood outside the house,
I still felt a bit weird. My clothes were really tight and I was
really bloated. My period was due the next day, so I put it down
to that.

The next morning, I woke up with an odd, metallic taste in my mouth. I felt a little bit peaky, not like I was going to be sick, but just not quite right. I went to the bathroom and sat on the loo, expecting my period to have come, but there was nothing at all.

And that's when it hit me: I was pregnant.

I think I was in shock because I was surprisingly calm as I pulled on my clothes and walked down to the local chemist to pick up a test. It made perfect sense. I felt tired, bloated and generally off colour and now my period – which by that point ran like clockwork, every twenty-eight days – was late.

It was almost like I didn't have to even take the test. I already knew. Some girls in my position might have gone through a period of denial, but I didn't have any of that. As I got back to the bathroom, unwrapped the test and peed on the little stick, I didn't even feel nervous as the two blue lines popped up. I just thought: how quickly can I get rid of this?

I know an abortion is not something you should do willy-nilly, but I think I'd become so numb and empty that I wasn't capable of feeling anything for the life growing inside me. It was just a problem, and it needed to be dealt with. If I was being truly honest with myself, I was just surprised it hadn't happened before now.

Now it amazes me how practical I was. Immediately as I held the little stick in my hand, all I could think of was how I needed to act, and fast. There were just two hurdles in my way: how would I tell Mum, and how would I tell Omar?

Of course, I knew the baby probably wasn't Omar's, but it suited me to pretend it was. In reality, the father could have been any one of about fifteen or twenty men. Omar was an outside bet. It was more likely to be Beaver's, or Mr Khan's. Or was it the Chinese man I saw every week, or the fat man from the hotel? The possibilities were numerous. The idea of going into labour without even knowing what race my baby would come out as didn't bear thinking about. I wasn't willing to take a chance.

In the end, I blurted it out to Mum, just like that, when she came in from work that night. I braced myself for her to scream and cry and break down but I was surprised by how reasonable she was. She gave me a hug and asked me what I wanted to do.

'We'll support you whatever decision you make,' she promised.

I told her my mind was already made up. There would be no baby. I was so determined to deal with it as quickly as possible, and get back to pretending it had never happened, that I didn't even tell Carly. I told Omar that I planned to have an abortion in the same breath that I told him I was pregnant, and I saw shock and relief written all over his face at the same time. It was unthinkable that he could go to his parents and tell them I was his girlfriend, let alone that I was pregnant. I think, deep down, he also knew there was a chance it wasn't his, though he never said as much.

We made an appointment with the doctor and I was sent to Birmingham for a scan. Mum came with me on the train and the lady who scanned me said I was seven weeks and two days gone and did I want to go away and think about my options?

But I had already thought about it and I knew exactly what I was going to do. Even when she gave me the timescale, it didn't narrow things down. I was so numb to everything that I couldn't even think back to the week the baby was supposed to have been conceived. I didn't even attempt to figure out who I'd slept with that week. I just went straight back the next day and told them I was sure I wanted to go ahead with the termination.

They told me it might feel really uncomfortable, but I was surprised by how easy it was. It wasn't painful and I didn't bleed much; I just had a few light spots.

Not that I had time to dwell on it. It wasn't long before my phone was ringing, with another call from Kev.

16

The Worst Night

Kev drove me to the takeaway where I'd slept with the Bangladeshi man who'd taken Viagra. Despite saying he'd never go back there, because of the row they'd had over money, we'd been going there a lot recently. Sometimes it was that man, and sometimes it was others.

I didn't tell Kev I'd had an abortion. What would have been the point? He'd have only told me he didn't care and that I was to get on with it. Instead, I told him I was on my period, so he gave me some of his sponges to soak up the blood.

I had no idea how dangerous it was to have sex so soon after what I'd been through, let alone to shove one of those ridiculous sponges into my body. I just shut off, as usual, and got on with it, as yet another nameless man climbed on top of me and did what he'd paid to do.

It's incredible to think that a few days later, I started my exams. Somehow, God knows how, I managed to actually concentrate on them. I didn't do much revision but I knew enough to get by.

I think I'd done two exams when Natalie texted to ask if I wanted to go to the pub with her for a drink. It was the day before bank holiday Monday. She said she knew some guys who would buy us drinks and it sounded like a laugh. I was in a bit of a mood because I'd been meant to meet Omar but his parents had dragged him off to a family thing at the last minute and he'd cancelled. So I said yes.

Despite the fact that Natalie swore all the time, and bragged about who she'd shagged, it was really laid-back at first. We played some pool and had a bit of a laugh. Some older Asian men came and joined us, but they seemed harmless. Natalie was drinking vodka, but I stuck to orange juice because I knew I had another exam in a few days' time.

We went on from there to another pub and one of the men persuaded me to have a real drink; just one wouldn't hurt me, would it? I can't even remember how old he was, or what he looked like, but I let him buy me an alcopop, a vodka and orange drink called Reef, which came in a little glass bottle.

For all I'd been through, I was still really naive in some respects, so when I needed the loo, I thought nothing of leaving my bottle of Reef on the table beside Natalie. I thought the worst someone could do to your drink was spit in it.

How wrong I was.

The room started to spin almost as soon as I took another sip. I didn't feel drunk; the sensation was different. My body felt limp, like a rag doll's. I could feel myself sliding slowly down the side of the table, losing control of my limbs and spilling the remains of my Reef on the floor. I tried to cry out, to tell Natalie that I thought something was wrong, really wrong, but no words would come out. I couldn't speak.

Things started to get really hazy, so I'm not sure how long

it was before Andy appeared, but the next thing I knew he and the other men were carrying me out to a waiting car. I couldn't even hold my head up and I was so, so dizzy. They put me in the back seat and draped me half over Natalie, half over another of the men, before they started to drive.

That's when they took off my trousers, and my knickers.

Although my memory of that awful night is very cloudy, I remember exactly what I was wearing: a black bra and knickers, tight-fitting black trousers, a black V-neck and a fitted green fleece.

I'm not sure where my trousers and knickers were when I was carried from the car into a house, naked from the waist down. They dumped me on the floor in the lounge and asked me if I wanted any more alcohol. I tried to shake my head but it just wouldn't move and I slumped down by the side of the couch.

I think I lost consciousness briefly, because the next thing I remember is being upstairs, in a bedroom, with Andy's face in mine. I was stark naked now. I seemed to have lost my V-neck and fleece and my bra along with my trousers and knickers. I can't remember much about the room except that it wasn't much different from the rooms I was usually taken to, with their mouldy walls and sparse, rotten furniture.

I couldn't focus on Andy, though his eyes were boring into me – huge, black, angry eyes, even more angry than Mr Khan's. There was a sea of faces around him, all laughing, goading me, mocking me, but I didn't know what was funny or what I was supposed to have done because I couldn't make out what they were saying or even if they were speaking English.

It was like my head was underwater and their voices were filtering down from above the surface.

I fell back on the mattress, still limp like a rag doll. I wanted so badly to get up and run, run as fast as I could, away from these men and this room and this bed, but I couldn't even raise my head or sit up.

Andy grabbed me by the shoulders and I knew he was digging his nails into my flesh but I couldn't feel a thing. Suddenly his voice seemed louder than the rest, rising above the noise.

He said: 'This is for my son. You've been having sex with my son, you little slut.'

If I could have spoken, I'd have said, no, I hadn't had sex with his son. I hadn't even given him a blow job. But I was still struck dumb, so I couldn't protest. Two of the men pinned my legs down as Andy climbed on top of me and another two held down my arms. As he started to rape me, everything went black.

When I regained consciousness, another of the men was on top of me. I think that's when the feeling in my lower half started to return a fraction, and I gave a weak little kick. But they told me not to kick off or it would take even longer. One by one they came to me, taking turns to rape me and pin me down, always rotating. With each man I got a little more feeling back and the pain started to take hold. I knew I was bleeding, because they were so rough, but I couldn't do anything to stop it. I tried to kick out again, but of course it was pointless. I was a weak, drugged, sixteen-year-old girl, and around me were eight, possibly nine, grown men.

'Fucking pack it in,' Andy said. By now, he was holding down my left leg, the one I'd tried to kick out with. 'Or we'll throw you out on the street with no clothes on.'

It was only then I realised I was crying. I started to regain the feeling in my face and the tears slipped down my cheeks and onto my naked body. All I could think was how much I'd rather be on the street naked than lying on this bed being gang-raped.

Finally the last of them finished. As soon as he climbed off me, I stumbled from the bed and managed to find the door. My legs were still like jelly and I couldn't walk in a straight line. I fell a couple of times, as I made my way out onto the landing, but of course nobody helped me up. I half-ran, half-fell into the bathroom and closed the door behind me.

I slid down the wall and started to sob harder than I ever had done before – huge, throaty, breathless sobs. My tears were coming thick and fast now and they blinded me as the blood running down my legs gathered in a pool beneath me. This felt so different to everything that had happened before. Before, I could at least trick myself into believing I had some sort of control over what was going on, but here I couldn't even pretend. It was the most frightening thing that had ever happened to me.

One of them rapped on the door and, through my tears, I told him to fuck off.

'Oh, come on,' he said. 'Don't be like that. It's not that bad.'

I couldn't believe what I was hearing. It was like I'd got in a huff over something ridiculous, like someone forgetting to text me back. I asked him to bring me my clothes and he said he'd get me a towel.

He never came back, so I just sat on the cold floor, bleeding and crying, and wondering what the hell I was going to do. Eventually I saw a small towel hanging from a rail near the toilet. It was tiny, and it would barely cover me up, but it was my only option because there was no chance they were giving me my clothes back.

The towel was really minging. It had obviously been used loads of times and never washed, but I didn't care. I wrapped it around me and it just covered me, but I was past caring about my modesty, so I just ran down the stairs and out of the front door, screaming and screaming and screaming.

My legs still weren't working properly, so I fell onto the hard, stone path. It was pitch-black and I had absolutely no idea what time it was. Although it was May, the night air was cold and I started to shiver as it hit me. Somehow – I'm still not quite sure how – my phone was in my hand, but it was completely dead.

Across the road, a woman was looking out of her window. She was about thirty, with a kind face. Before I knew it, she'd sprinted across the street and was kneeling beside me, taking my hand and telling me to come inside with her. I did as she said, and she asked me what the hell had happened, was I OK, could she ring the police? She really thought we ought to ring the police.

She took me into her house and there were toys and baby bottles all around. Her husband was standing in the kitchen and I could see the shock spreading across his face as he saw me. I didn't blame him for looking so aghast. It's not every day a teenage girl stumbles naked and bleeding into your kitchen in the middle of the night.

'I've been up with my baby,' the woman explained. 'I thought I saw you being carried into the house earlier on, but I assumed you'd maybe just had a bit too much to drink. I kept an eye out, though, something just didn't seem quite right. Don't you think we should ring the police, Paul?'

Her husband nodded. 'Definitely, we definitely should.'

'No!' I cried. 'No, no, please don't. Please don't. I just want some clothes.'

They gave each other a little look, as if they didn't really know what to do, but the woman went upstairs and got me a jumper and some trousers. She kept talking about the police and I kept telling her no, I didn't want to talk to the police, I just wanted to go home.

What would Andy and the other men do to me if I told the police? It didn't bear thinking about.

The woman asked me if I wanted to at least ring my mum, but I phoned Omar instead. He answered sleepily and, as I told him I'd been raped by his friend's dad and lost all of my clothes, I started to cry again.

The line went really, really quiet before he said: 'I'll speak to you in the morning.'

I was devastated by his reaction. I guess at just sixteen he simply didn't know how to deal with the enormity of what I'd told him, and the consequences in his community were so far-reaching, but I couldn't understand that back then, and it tore me apart that he couldn't acknowledge what I'd just told him.

'Paul will give you a lift home,' the woman said gently. 'Where do you live?'

It was only then I realised I had no idea where I was. I guessed

I was still in Telford, but I'd never been to this street before, so I didn't know which part. One thing I was certain of was that I didn't want a lift home from Paul. He seemed all right but there was no way I was taking the chance of getting into another strange car, alone, with another strange man. I told them no, I'd be fine, but asked them where I was. Reluctantly they told me I was in one of the villages just outside the town, but they really didn't want me to try to walk home. I know now they meant well, but I was almost hysterical with paranoia, thinking now they were going to lock me in their house, so I begged to be let out.

At the bottom of the street was a phone box, so I ran towards it. I had no money but someone had shown me a trick once where you can punch in a code and ring a number and you get two seconds before it cuts out. I dialled Beaver's number and he answered, his voice groggy.

'It's me,' I said. 'Ring me on this number.'

He did as I asked and I sobbed again, as I told him what I'd told Omar, that I'd been raped and I'd lost all of my clothes. I was starting to get really sore down below now and I winced in pain as I asked him to pick me up. Surely, after everything we'd done together, he'd at least come and pick me up?

'Holly, forget it,' he said. 'I'm sleeping. It's the middle of the night.'

Even Beaver didn't care enough to rescue me, so my only option was to walk home, or rather run. My legs still felt really weird but I sprinted through miles of fields and dark alleyways, thinking of nothing but the blood gushing down my legs. As I got closer to home, I bumped into two lads who had been a couple of years above me at school.

'Hey!' one of them said. 'Woah, you OK? What are you doing out so late on your own?'

'Just leave me alone!' I screamed. 'Don't even touch me.'

Eventually my street slid into view and I slowed to a halt. I still didn't know what time it was, so I thought it would be best to try to creep back in. I wasn't thinking straight and somehow I told myself that Mum might not have noticed I hadn't come home.

I slowly pulled the door handle down, praying it would be open, as God knows where my keys were. Mum was sitting at the kitchen table, her white face etched with worry. The clock on the wall read half past three.

As she looked me up and down, she said, 'I've been ringing you all night. Where the hell have you been? And where are your clothes?'

17

Rock Bottom

Mum was fuming. She went on and on and on about how worried she'd been and how many times she'd tried to ring me. She kept asking about my clothes, so I lied and said I'd spilled a drink down myself and Natalie had lent me some of her stuff to go home in. She knew it was a load of rubbish and she told me I was grounded.

For once, I was actually really relieved. I knew Kev and Mr Khan wouldn't be at all happy that I wasn't able to come out, but I just couldn't deal with them so, for once, I was willing to take that chance. I'd never been happier than I was to go shopping with Mum the next day.

I'd only had a few hours in bed but I hardly slept a wink. Every time I closed my eyes, all I could see was Andy and the sea of angry, jeering faces. I was still bleeding loads and I had to wear a pad in my knickers, as if I had my period. I was in loads of pain but I took a couple of paracetamol and hoped the nauseating aches would soon ease off.

Mum knew something wasn't right. As we walked through town, she kept asking me loads of questions about the night before. Part of me wanted to tell her, but another part of me couldn't bear to say it out loud because then it would all become real again.

We were just coming out of one shop when I caught sight of one of the lads I'd seen when I'd been running home the night before. My heart almost stopped as I saw him walking towards me. I tried to pretend I hadn't seen him but it was too late.

'Hey!' he said, concern in his eyes. 'Are you OK?'

Mum looked at me, suspicion written all over her face. 'Fine,' I snapped.

'Did you get home OK last night?' the boy went on, and I hoped he could see that my eyes were pleading with him to shut the hell up.

'Yes, fine, thanks,' I said, and turned to walk off without another word. The lad gave a confused shrug and walked off, leaving me to answer even more of Mum's questions.

'Were you with those boys last night?' she said. 'Were you drinking?'

'No,' I said. 'I've never seen them before in my life. They must be getting mixed up.'

From there, we went to do the weekly shop at Morrisons. Mum asked me to go and get her a trolley while she bought some juice for Lauren and Amy to keep them quiet. As I walked up to the little booth, I saw something that made my whole body tense in fear.

Andy.

He was sitting in his car with the window down, as if he'd been waiting for me, and waiting to get me on my own. Just the sight of his face was enough to make me feel dizzy and sick, and for a moment I thought I might throw up. How did he know

I'd be here? He sat there, just looking at me for a few seconds, before he summoned me over.

It was broad daylight and the car park was busy with shoppers, but I still wondered if he might pull me back into the car and take me to the awful house from the night before, so I froze. He said my name again, more forcefully this time, and I started to shake as I walked towards the car. I stopped a few yards away, still frightened to get too close.

'Don't you fucking dare say anything about what happened last night,' he hissed, voice lowered. 'I'm fucking warning you.'

Then he rolled his window up and drove off. I had to grab hold of another car so I didn't collapse in a heap on the tarmac.

Hoping beyond hope, I convinced myself that was the last I'd hear from Andy, but I was wrong. Very wrong. When I got home that evening, a strange number flashed up on my phone, as I sat alone in my room, trying to stop the images of the night before from running through my brain for what felt like the millionth time. When I answered it, I instantly recognised his deep, menacing voice.

'Look out of your front window,' he said.

My palms were sweaty as I walked across the room and pulled back the curtains to see Andy sitting in his car. I had no idea how he'd found out my address but it didn't matter. He knew where I lived and where my family lived.

He gave me a sick little wave so I instinctively pulled the curtains shut again and slid down the wall in terror.

'Do you remember Lucy Lowe, Holly?' he asked. 'You must have heard of Lucy Lowe.'

Everyone in Telford knew who Lucy Lowe was. She'd only been around my age when she'd become involved with a twenty-six-year-old taxi driver called Azhar Ali Mehmood. He'd set her house on fire, killing her and also her mother and sister.

'Did you hear me, Holly?' he said. 'I asked if you'd heard of Lucy Lowe.'

I was almost convulsing in fear now and Andy seemed to think it was funny, listening to me struggling to get air into my lungs.

'Yes,' I said between gasps. I wanted to cry but I felt like I was beyond tears.

'Well, if you're thinking of saying anything about this to anyone,' he said, 'remember that name. Lucy Lowe. That's all I'm saying.'

He hung up and left me hyperventilating on my bedroom floor.

Over the next week or so, the threats continued. If Andy wasn't outside my house, looking up into my room, he was on the other end of the phone, calmly whispering threats. I think he realised how terrified I was of my house being set on fire, so he played on that, but he also threatened to hurt my little sisters, which would always send me into a blind, hysterical panic. He never really raised his voice, which somehow made him all the more frightening.

'I will rape them,' he'd say. 'You know that's not a threat. It's a promise.'

Lauren was just six and Amy only four. How could he even

contemplate doing something so depraved? But this man was pure evil. He scared me even more than Mr Khan did, and that was really saying something.

I was so withdrawn and shaky that Mum refused to accept there was nothing wrong with me. The slightest noise would have me jumping out of my skin and, every night, I crept downstairs four or five times, terrified that Andy had posted a petrol bomb through my letterbox.

In the end, she sat me down and begged me to tell her what had happened. After stuttering and muttering and trying my best to skirt around the subject, I eventually blurted out that I'd been raped. I didn't tell her who it was, though, or how many men were involved.

Mum was absolutely gutted, and kept apologising to me for being so angry. She was crying and telling me we had to phone the police, we had to do something, but I told her I couldn't handle it and to leave me alone so I could concentrate on my exams. She wasn't happy about it, but agreed to let me focus on my GCSEs.

As I hadn't been allowed out, the calls from Mr Khan and Kev had been coming thick and fast. They were both really angry but I just tried to ignore them. I didn't have to walk to or from school, unless I had an exam, and even then I was never there at my normal time, so they didn't know where to find me, unless they walked straight up to my front door.

Which is exactly what Mr Khan did.

I was upstairs in my room, trying my best to revise, poring over maths equations that made my head swim, when I saw him coming up the garden path in his familiar grubby white robes. Things seemed to happen in slow motion, as he reached for the letterbox and put something in. I jumped to my feet and tore down the stairs, terrified he'd posted a petrol bomb through the door. I could almost taste the smoke, as I imagined the house going up in flames with my whole family inside. My whole family was going to die, and all because I'd been such a slag.

By the time I got to the bottom of the stairs, Liam had already got to the letter. He was home from university for a few days. I jumped up and down, trying to grab it from him, but he wouldn't let it go.

'This guy says you're a prostitute,' he said, eyes widening in disgust. 'And that you owe him loads of money. Is that true?'

I felt like time had suddenly stopped. Mr Khan had always threatened to tell Mum I was a prostitute if I didn't do what he said, and now he'd followed through with his threat.

My hands shook, as an awful reality dawned on me: if he could do the unthinkable, so could Andy.

I think it was in that moment that I decided my life was no longer worth living. The next few minutes were chaos, as Liam summoned Mum and she read Mr Khan's spidery, misspelled note in utter disbelief. She told me to phone Carly and get her to come round, which I did, as if I was on autopilot.

'What?' Carly said. 'How did she find out? How does she know?'

'Just come round,' I said flatly. I didn't know what I hoped she'd do or say.

The colour drained from Carly's face as Mum started to quiz her on whether or not I was a prostitute, and if I owed Mr Khan money, and what the hell this was all about. She stuttered that he must be making it all up because it definitely wasn't true, but Mum knew something was going on, something far more serious than I'd ever let on.

How could I have caused her such pain and humiliation? I couldn't live with the guilt, and neither could I live with the constant fear that Andy was going to turn up in the middle of the night and kill my family as they slept. I genuinely believed I was better off dead and that my family would be safer if I was gone.

I wanted to do one last thing to make Mum proud so I decided I'd wait until after exams had finished before I killed myself. She could open my results when I was dead and gone, and she could tell people that at least I'd worked hard and passed everything and my life hadn't been one big fuck-up.

My last exam was IT and it was the following Friday. I spent the next few days holed up in my room, pretending to be studying, but really writing letters to everyone telling them how sorry I was and how much I loved them, but I couldn't go on. I explained what had been happening to me and told them I hoped they understood, but that I could see why they might not. There was a note for Mum and Dad, one for each of my siblings, and one for Omar and Carly. They were the only people who mattered in my life, but I honestly felt that their lives would be much better if I wasn't there. Tears dripped from my eyes onto the white paper as I said my goodbyes, then sealed the envelopes shut.

When Friday came, I was strangely calm. I got through my exam quite easily. I guessed I might have even done quite well, but of course I'd never know because I'd be long gone before the results came out. When I said goodbye to Jenny and the other girls at the gates, I felt a little sad and I wondered what they'd say when they found out I was dead. They'd probably come to my funeral and hug Mum and tell her they had no idea, which of course would be the truth.

There was only one thing I wanted to do and that was to see Omar one last time. I phoned him and asked him to meet me in town. Things had been a bit strained between us since the incident with Andy and all the other men, but that didn't seem to matter anymore. I just wanted to say goodbye. We were only together for quarter of an hour but as he hugged me goodbye, I took his face in my hands and gave him a soft kiss on the lips. He looked a bit shocked, as we hardly ever kissed anymore, but he didn't object. As we turned and walked in separate directions, I felt the smallest tinge of sadness that he'd never hug or kiss me again.

That evening was one of the longest of my life. I'd decided I was going to wait until everyone had gone to bed to over-dose, because then there was less chance of them finding me and trying to stop me. Mum had a medicine box in the kitchen where she kept lots of painkillers, and I'd had a quick look the previous evening. There were dozens of pills there and I planned to take them all. I'd bought some stomach salts from the chemist, to make sure I didn't throw up. I wanted to be certain all of the poison stayed in my system. I'd also managed to buy a mini bottle of vodka from the corner shop, using the cash from Kev I still had under my floorboard.

This was no cry for help. I really, really wanted to die.

Around ten, everyone went to bed while I calmly went to the medicine box and counted out all of the pills I could find. There were nearly eighty paracetamol tablets there, and I fully intended to take them all. I opened all of the packaging and carefully placed it in bins all over the house. On the off chance that I did survive for a little while, I didn't want anyone to know how many I'd taken as I didn't want them to try to treat me properly. I just wanted this all to be over.

I took the pills first. I didn't even take a drink of water to wash them down; I just swallowed them dry, each one sticking in my throat as I tried to force it down. I'm not sure how long it took but I waited until every pill in the house was gone. Then I took the stomach salts and washed them down with a few massive glugs of vodka. It was so strong it burned my mouth and I almost gagged, but I managed to swallow it.

It was only as I climbed the stairs that I started to feel a little woozy, but I put on my pyjamas and found my way into bed. I took some headphones out of my school bag and placed them in my ears, hoping some music would help me drift off to sleep.

I shuffled through some tracks and found my favourite song, but it wasn't something mellow and soothing. It was 'Always on Time' by Ja Rule and Ashanti which, ironically, was all about sex. As I settled down for the end, I put it on repeat and let the lyrics reverberate around my brain. Then, I closed my eyes and waited for death to take hold.

It was the retching which woke me first. I sat bolt upright in my bed, as I realised I wasn't dead, at least not yet. It was still dark outside and the light from the street lamps was pouring into my room. Drenched in cold sweat, I was trying to be sick. My body was trying to rid itself of the poison I'd fed it, but the stomach salts seemed to be doing the trick and keeping it all down. My stomach contracted violently as I gasped in pain. I just hoped Mum didn't hear me. I didn't want anyone to come into my room or to come to my aid. I just wanted it all to be over.

Before long, the room was swimming before my eyes. I was drifting out of consciousness again. I prayed that this time when I closed my eyes it would be for good.

It felt like just seconds before my stomach contracted again. I was sitting up straight, retching loudly once more, but now it was light. Hours must have passed and I could only hope that I was now beyond help, that it was only a matter of time before I slipped away. I'd thought it might be painless and peaceful, that I'd just drift into oblivion as my music played softly in my ears. I hadn't bargained on how hard my body would fight to stay alive.

I heard Mum's footsteps on the landing and fresh sweat soaked my body. I turned away from the door, hoping she'd assume I was asleep, but she walked straight in and up to my bed, where I lay facing the wall.

'You don't sound well,' she said. 'Were you sick just there?'

I mumbled something about maybe having a bug but my speech must have been slurred because suddenly Mum's expression changed. She grabbed me by the shoulders and turned my face around to see I'd gone completely grey and my lips were blue. There was a flash of sheer terror in her eyes as she let out a piercing scream.

'Oh my God!' she roared. 'You stupid girl! You stupid,

stupid girl! Get up, now, we need to get you to hospital! Why have you done this? Why?'

She threw open my bedroom door and started screaming and screaming. Phil came running to the foot of the stairs and she ordered him to call an ambulance. He was so stressed he had to ask Mum what the number was. I made it halfway downstairs before I slumped in a heap in my pyjamas. I couldn't hear much. I felt like I was underwater and my vision was really blurred, but in the distance I could hear *The Powerpuff Girls* playing on TV, as Mum hastily turned it up and told Lauren and Amy everything would be fine, I just wasn't too well but the doctors were coming to fix me and they'd not to worry.

She was running in and out of every room in the house, each time with another empty packet in her hands, begging me to tell her how many pills I'd taken. I was beyond speech. Even if I'd wanted her to save me, I couldn't form the words. My brain felt like it was slowly shutting down as things got hazier and hazier.

It was only a matter of minutes before the sound of sirens filled the air and blue lights shone into our once-quiet lounge.

I was in hospital for a week but I don't remember most of it. When the doctors tried to pump my stomach, I had an allergic reaction to some of the medicine. I had to have lots of injections and I was on oxygen but it was all a bit of a blur. Mum and the rest of the family must have been really worried but I was still in a daze. As I'd tried to kill myself, I had to see a psychiatrist. I wasn't allowed to see her on my own – Mum and Dad had to be there too – so of course there was no way I was going to tell her half of what was going on in my life. I simply said I'd been raped, just once, and it had all been too much but I was fine now.

I wasn't fine, far from it. I was still very mixed up and confused and I didn't know whether I should be happy I was still alive with a family who loved me, or upset that it wasn't all over like I'd planned. As I lay in hospital, mulling over the mess that had become my life, the ward sister stopped by my bed to read my chart. As she did, she narrowed her eyes and stared at me, still with my oxygen mask around my face, helpless and lost.

'You're a silly girl,' she said, shaking her head with a tut. 'Just looking for attention, I bet. Well, I hope you hurry up and get better soon – but only because having you here is a waste of our time and our money. We really could be doing with getting that bed back.'

18

Escape

After my suicide attempt, I was told I had to go to counselling with my family. I didn't speak about anything that had happened to me. I wanted to curl up in a ball and pretend none of it had ever happened. I mumbled a few things about being raped once but that was it. Then I was sent back home, as if nothing had ever happened, back to my old life and all its trappings.

One thing that did change was that I didn't get picked up by Mr Khan anymore. I think he'd got bored of me. Maybe I was becoming too old for him, or maybe he felt like he'd lost some of his power over me now that he'd gone and told Mum I was a prostitute like he'd always threatened to do. He didn't know I'd tried to kill myself, so maybe he thought his letter hadn't had any effect. Mum certainly never gave him any money and neither did I.

Instead, he sold my phone number to a student from Afghanistan who picked me up occasionally instead. He did sleep with me, in exchange for driving lessons, but he was nowhere near as bad as Mr Khan. He was actually OK to talk to, just a bit lonely, and he didn't smell horrendous, which was a huge bonus. In my crazy, mixed-up mind I thought I was actually getting quite a good deal.

It wasn't so easy cutting ties with Kev, though. He still had a weird sort of authority over me, as if he was my dad or something. I just felt compelled to do as he said, as I'd been following his orders for so long. He continued to take me to the Chinese man on Tuesdays and anyone else he could find. I remember sleeping with a horrible man who asked me to take my jewellery off because he had a water bed. As we lay down on it, he breathed his coffee and fag breath in my face, and told me how nice it was to lie beside a girl and not a woman. He made me sick, but I was a zombie, still sleepwalking through the nightmare.

Miraculously, I'd managed to pass all of my GCSEs, despite being suicidal and doing barely any revision. I got an A in travel and tourism and Bs and Cs in everything else. I even got a B in IT, despite the fact I'd been hours from attempting suicide when I sat the exam.

My teachers told me my grades were good enough to get me into sixth-form college, and maybe even university, but I was still living day to day. The little girl who dreamed of being an air hostess and travelling the world had left for good the night Andy had taken me to that house, and I wasn't sure if she'd ever return.

Despite everything, I decided to go on to college to do a diploma in travel and tourism, mainly because I couldn't face being stuck in the house with my thoughts and memories. It was only a few weeks after I started that a familiar feeling returned.

I was wrestling with my jeans one morning, trying with all my might to pull them up, when I realised they wouldn't fasten at the top. I tried another pair, and another, but none would fit over my stomach. I was so bloated I had to go out and buy a pair of jogging bottoms.

I just knew.

I knew before I'd calculated when my next period was due that I was pregnant again. I had the same metallic taste in my mouth, the same dizzy feeling. It had happened again, and again I didn't have a clue who the dad was or even what race he was.

All I wanted to do was get rid of it, but I couldn't get a scan in Birmingham for a few weeks so they sent me to Chester, which was a bit further north, just over an hour away by train. I went on my own this time and, after my scan, I walked around the shops in a daze, looking at clothes like nothing had happened. When I came home, I switched my phone off. I didn't even want to speak to Omar because our relationship was in freefall.

'Why do you have a password on your phone?' he'd asked, a few nights before. 'Why do you never leave it alone for two minutes? Are you cheating on me?'

Things just hadn't been the same since I'd overdosed, and I guess he felt guilty for not trying harder when I'd told him I'd been raped, but the situation was getting too big for two teenagers to handle.

I was eight weeks pregnant by the time I was given an appointment for the actual termination, in Birmingham. In my heart of hearts, I knew the baby wasn't Omar's. The chances were minimal. We barely held hands anymore, let alone slept together. Ironically Mum had softened a bit towards him since my suicide attempt, and she'd let him come round to the house, although he wasn't allowed to stay over. I guess she assumed the baby was his because a few nights before the abortion she sat me down in the kitchen and told me to think carefully about what I was about to do.

'I think you need to think carefully about this, Holly,' she said. 'Do you really want to go through with this?'

I nodded my head.

'But it's the second time it's happened,' Mum went on. 'Maybe your body is trying to tell you something? You do know we'd support you, don't you? I think you're just so messed up by this rape; maybe you should have some more counselling. What do you think?'

'I've decided, Mum,' I replied. 'I'm having another abortion.'

If truth be told, the only emotion I felt was disappointment. I was disappointed in myself for getting into this mess again, because I still firmly believed it was my fault. No one had ever told me about contraception, not properly, and I didn't realise I had options. I guess if I'd gone ahead and had the baby I would have loved him or her, but I couldn't imagine anything about it and I didn't want to. I just wanted it gone, for all traces of my abuse to be sucked out of my womb.

It was only after the operation that I realised I'd got off fairly lightly the first time. I bled so much and it was so painful I thought my insides were falling out. I rang the clinic and they told me it was normal but I couldn't settle. Eventually I passed everything I was supposed to pass but it was an uncomfortable few days.

I think it was then that I made the conscious decision to make myself unattractive. I stopped bleaching my hair and wearing trendy clothes. I hid away in the jogging bottoms I'd bought for the brief few weeks of my pregnancy and I ate and I ate and I ate.

Carly hadn't had to do half the stuff I had because she was fat. Maybe if I made myself fat too, I'd become less of a target. I knew I had a long way to go, but I'd try my bloody best to get as big as I could.

Put simply, I'd just lost all respect for my body. It didn't feel like my own anymore, so why should I try to do right by it? I stuffed myself with sweets and crisps and takeaways, and things only got easier when I turned seventeen and moved into a flat with Gemma. As well as studying for my diploma course, I took on a part-time job in Morrisons, where I could buy all the food I wanted with my staff discount. I went up a dress size or two and I looked really bloated, especially compared to how I used to be, but I was still by no means obese.

Kev wasn't put off, at least not enough to stop taking me out. But it became harder for me to meet him. I was getting loads of hours in the supermarket, which he wasn't happy about, especially when it meant I didn't have time to do Tuesday nights with the Chinese man. I was nervous about pissing Kev off, but somehow I found the strength to stand my ground and he started to work around my job, always huffing and puffing like I was doing him a huge favour.

Little did I know he had expanded his sordid venture.

One night, he took me to a filthy house and there were several men there. It was no different from usual, except another girl was there. She said her name was Maria, but that was about all I could make out, because she had a bad speech impediment. She looked younger than me and it was obvious from speaking to her that she had learning difficulties. It made me sick to my stomach to think how easy it must have been for Kev to lure her in, but what could I do?

One night, I was walking out of work, when a taxi pulled up at the side of the road and an Asian driver leaned out of the window.

'Hey,' he said. 'Hey!'

I folded my arms and said nothing, wondering what kind of request he would have for me.

Instead, he said, 'I know what's happening to you. It's no secret and it's not right. I can help you.'

'It's fine,' I mumbled. 'I don't need your help.'

'Listen,' he said. He had kind eyes, and looked around fifty. 'I don't want anything from you, I promise. I just want this to stop. It's happening to too many young girls and it's not right. I can give you a new sim card for your phone. Throw the old one away. Please.'

I pulled up the zip on my green work fleece to shield my face. Just another older man, promising not to hurt me but to help me. How could I trust him? How could I trust any man?

'No,' I said. 'Thank you, but I don't need a new sim card.'

'Please,' he said. 'Just let me give you this. I won't even take the number.'

But I was already picking up the pace, walking away as fast as I could.

In the end, my escape came gradually. I was still seeing Beaver a lot and I still struggled to accept he wasn't really my friend, even when he took me to Birmingham one night and tried to sell me to some men he'd met in a casino. Even though he now had Maria, Kev still took me out whenever he could. I suppose, in the end, I realised the only option was to move away.

Before that, the inevitable happened. Omar broke up with me. He told me it wasn't working and I told him to fuck off. Within weeks, he was going out with someone else. I just didn't care. There was a time when I'd have been devastated, but now I just wanted to leave Telford and all of its bad memories behind.

I looked online and found a room to rent in Birmingham. It wasn't as far away as I'd have liked, but at least it wasn't Telford. Carly agreed to come with me and share the room, so we could save money on rent. I eventually did as the taxi driver said and got a new sim card, although I was too scared to throw the old one away just yet.

I worked a variety of shop jobs and I went on some dates, but I didn't know how to behave around men who hadn't paid for me, so I often ended up sleeping with them on the first night – but this was far better than being bought and sold and at least I got to choose this time.

It was around six months before I met Sanjeev in an internet chatroom. He was an Indian medical student in Scotland and we gradually started talking and getting to know each other. He respected me and it was ages before we even met in person, never mind slept together.

By this time, it was getting a bit much sharing a room with Carly every night, and when Sanjeev got his first job, in Oxford, I moved there with him and worked in Waitrose. It felt so good to be miles away from home and, for a while, I imagined we'd grow old there, just Sanjeev and me against the world.

At this time, I was barely speaking to anyone in my family, apart from Gemma. She was the only one who didn't seem spooked by how much I'd been through and we could actually talk quite openly about it. Liam was another story, however. He didn't want to know about any of it. I guess he couldn't handle the idea of something so horrific happening to his little sister, so he pretended it hadn't happened at all. I knew things were hard for him, but it really drove a wedge between us.

As for Mum, I suppose I was a bit resentful towards her. I knew she loved me and that she hadn't known what I was going through, but for a few years I was very angry at her and I felt like she should have picked up on the signs. We kept in touch and I popped home for birthdays and at Christmas, but I rarely phoned home unless it was an emergency and I'd use any excuse for not being in touch.

Sanjeev and I were together for a year and a half and most of it was happy. I did tell him about my past, but I said I'd been a prostitute because I still didn't really understand what had happened. Eventually I think it drove a bit of a wedge between us, because Sanjeev didn't really understand either and I was still very much wrestling with all of my demons and waking up in the middle of the night, gripped by nightmares. Gradually we drifted apart and, after just over eighteen months, we broke up.

Although it didn't work out, the relationship did help me get far away from Telford for long enough to put a stop to the hell that had become my life. The split wasn't too awful and I decided I felt strong enough to move back to Birmingham and apply for university. I decided I'd do business studies instead of tourism. I guess part of me still wanted to be an air hostess, to travel the world and to see things I'd dreamed of the very first time I'd got on that plane to Majorca. But, unsurprisingly, I'd lost my confidence. I'd even gone as far as getting an application form for an airline, but I lost my nerve at the last minute. It was my dream, but what if I was bad at it? I just couldn't cope with the idea of failing at it.

But before I did, there was just one more thing I had to do. I went home to Telford and put my old sim card back in my phone. As soon as it registered, the phone beeped with two-year-old messages from Beaver and Kev and lots of others.

I felt like the same girl in some ways, but I was a little stronger now. For all Sanjeev had struggled with what I'd told him, he'd shown me that I was worth more than the price these men had put on my head.

I'm not sure how I found the guts to do what I did next, but I dialled Beaver's number. When he answered, I didn't say hello or ask him how he was. Instead, I said: 'I want you to give me some money, or I'm going to tell your wife everything.'

19

Moving On

The tables had turned with Beaver and it felt good.

As soon as I threatened him he came to meet me straight away and pretty much offered to give me anything I wanted. He still had the same car and, as it crawled up to the side of the road near Mum's, the smell of pizzas wafted from the windows. When he got out, he was already counting out a wad of notes.

'Holly!' he said. 'Please, I will give you money but don't tell her. Please.'

It wasn't really about money, though. It was about power. He looked so pathetic as he begged me not to say a word that I couldn't help but feel a little sorry for him. I quickly turned and left, though. There was no way I was falling into the trap of becoming his friend again. A few days later, I left and my new life began, though the old one still cast a dark shadow.

When I moved to Birmingham, I met another Indian man, Indu. We worked in Tesco together and he was kind, caring and funny. We started dating soon afterwards and, a few years later, I fell pregnant. This time there was no doubt in my mind that I wanted to go through with the pregnancy. An abortion just wasn't even an option. From the second the two blue lines appeared on the test, I loved that baby with all my heart. Unlike my two teenage pregnancies, I started to picture her little face and think of what I might call her, of the songs I might sing to her and the games we might play together.

It meant I had to give up university, which was a shame, as I had been doing well, but I needed to make this little person my focus. My pregnancy was also the best thing that could have happened to me in terms of my relationship with my family. As soon as I told Mum, she was over the moon at the prospect of being a grandmother, and the girls, teenagers by now, couldn't wait to be aunties, as they thought it seemed really cool and grown-up.

Mum and I didn't have a big heart-to-heart about what had happened. We just accepted that we were going to be in each other's lives a bit more again and that was that. It was easier that way.

Nine months later, little Charlotte came along. As I stroked the tiny covering of dark hair on her head, and held her soft wrinkled hand in mine, my heart swelled with love. She was quite simply the most beautiful baby girl I'd ever seen in my life.

It was only then that I really thought about my own mum, and how she must have felt the same all those years ago when she took me in her arms for the first time, knowing nothing of what would happen to me in years to come. I already had so many hopes and dreams for this little baby, yet I'd brought her into a world where such evil existed. I vowed there and then to protect her as much as I could and to try to make the world a better place for her to live in.

Many of the men who'd raped me had daughters, too. Had they cradled their own little girls in their arms like I had? I was someone's little girl. How could they do what they did to someone else's baby, knowing they had one of their own?

Sadly, my relationship with Charlotte's dad broke down. There were a number of reasons and it's still quite strained. The long and short of it was, I decided to move back to Telford, to be closer to my family. I knew things would be better for Charlotte if we had Mum and my sisters and the rest of our support network around us.

Shortly before I moved back, the police had tracked me down as part of something called Operation Chalice. They were investigating claims of sexual abuse, rape and trafficking against a number of men in the area, mainly Pakistanis. Someone, I'm not sure who, had given them my name when they made inquiries. It took them months to track me down because, even in Birmingham, I had a habit of moving around a lot, still scared that one or more of my abusers would catch up with me and my life would unravel. In the early days, before Charlotte, I'd moved on average every six months, always looking over my shoulder.

When the police spoke to me, I agreed to be interviewed. I wasn't sure what to expect, but I thought it was best to give it a go. I'm not quite sure what happened but going back over the events of those awful days awakened strange feelings inside me. I told the police about Kev, and the officers looked at each other in shock, as he hadn't even been on their radar. I started to wonder if they'd just buried their heads in the sand because it had been simply too big a problem and they couldn't deal with it. How could they not have known? He was trafficking children so brazenly around the town, touting his services in takeaways and in the bookies. Were the police really so thick they hadn't noticed?

I really wanted to tell them all about Mr Khan, but I'm afraid to say they didn't seem too interested because they'd already picked him up on other charges. It was a very confusing time. I suppose the officers had a duty to prepare me for what I might face in court, so they tried to demonstrate to me what it might be like having all different barristers cross-examine me, telling me I was a liar and that I'd made it all up.

We had a bit of a mock trial and it was completely and utterly soul-destroying. I'm not ashamed to say I just couldn't cope with it. I doubt very few victims could. It's like reliving the worst days of your life over and over again, but this time it wouldn't be just the perpetrators sneering at me, it would be well-spoken men and women in wigs, too.

It's a difficult one, because I agree that everyone should be entitled to a fair trial if our justice system is to work – and part of that involves having a lawyer – but I can't help but think there must be another way for girls like me to get justice.

After we were done, I was in a very dark place for a few days. Although the horrors of the abuse would never leave me completely, I no longer spent every waking hour wishing I was dead, and I now had a life I actually quite liked.

'I can't do it,' I told the police. 'I can't go through this. I'm sorry.'

'We think you're really valuable to this case,' one officer said, when I explained my decision. 'Won't you think about reconsidering?'

But my mind was made up. I honestly felt like if I took that stand – and my abusers were lined up in the dock – I'd become suicidal again. I didn't just have my own life to think of – I had Charlotte to consider and I was a single mum. She needed me to get out of bed in the morning and feed her and clothe her and cuddle her. Could I do all of those things if I was crippled by the depression and fear that had almost claimed my life as a teenager? It just didn't seem worth the risk.

And what if they were found not guilty? It had been so long – what if there wasn't enough evidence? What if they all got off and then came looking for me? Would they still want to set my house on fire? Would they go after Charlotte?

Don't get me wrong – I have enormous respect for survivors of sexual abuse who stand up in court and testify against their perpetrators, but I don't think those who choose not to are nec-essarily weaker. We all face our battles in different ways and, until you've walked a mile in our shoes, you can't possibly say how you'd deal with what we've been through.

Instead of going through the courts, I decided to fight child sexual exploitation in another way. I started to blog about my past and I attended charity events, speaking to other survi-vors and sharing my story with them and with professionals. Eventually I got a job with a local charity in Telford that works with girls who are being abused like I was.

I don't want to talk about their cases. I'd never breach their confidentiality, and their stories aren't mine to tell. But I do try to persuade them that there is light at the end of the tunnel and it is possible to come out the other side. I only hope they believe me. Perhaps, if there had been a service like that when I was in the throes of abuse, it might have helped me understand my situation a bit better.

Now, I've met a new man. By the time you read this, I'll have given birth to my second child. It wasn't planned, more of a pleasant surprise, but I'm looking forward to it and Charlotte can't wait to have a little brother or sister.

For a long time, I couldn't see my future but now I'm living it – and that's something I feel very proud of.

Epilogue

If you see me in the street today, I look like any other woman in Telford. To the naked eye, I'm no different from the next working mum trying to make ends meet. Perhaps you'll see me on the school run, straightening my daughter's tie as she bounds through the gates, full of the joy and innocence that every child should feel for as long as they possibly can. Or maybe you'll see me rushing around town after a hard day's work, pushing my trolley around the supermarket, thinking of packed lunches and evening meals.

But behind closed doors, in the dead of night, I dream that I'm back there.

Sometimes, I dream that Andy or Mr Khan has come for my sisters like they promised, and their piercing screams are so real that I sit bolt upright in bed, begging for them to be let go. Other times I dream my house is on fire. I can see the flames and taste the smoke. The images flashing through my head are so powerful that there have been many times I've woken up drenched in sweat, shaking in utter terror.

The fear never goes away – you just have to learn to live with it, to piece your life together as best you can.

I suppose it doesn't help that so many of my abusers are still so close at hand.

Shortly after I left Telford, Mr Khan was convicted of raping a fifteen-year-old girl he picked up on the street, and indecently assaulting a woman in her early twenties. I didn't know who either was, but my heart ached for them as I imagined his horrible breath on their faces and his dirty hands grabbing their hair in the back of his cramped little car. He's been released now, and I still see him on the street, evil still shining out of his black eyes.

After I left for Birmingham, Beaver moved on to other girls. I heard on the grapevine that he sold them to his friends and colleagues, a bit like Kev had sold me. He was eventually picked up by the police and when he appeared in court on charges of controlling a child prostitute – I still loathe that term, as I believe there is no such thing, but that was the official wording – he pleaded guilty, as there was too much evidence stacked up against him. He was jailed.

Operation Chalice finally came to court in 2013, nearly three years after the police had first tried to track me down in Birmingham. Ali, or Mohammed Ali Sultan, was jailed for seven years. When he became an adult, he graduated from selling phone numbers to abusing teenage girls himself, except now he was an adult and they were still children. He admitted having sex with two teenage girls, one of whom was just thirteen at the time.

Mubarek Ali, who threw the bottle of piss at me when I refused to give him a blow job, was jailed for fourteen years. His brother, Ahdel, got eighteen. They were convicted of sexually abusing and trafficking four teenagers.

No one ever got Andy. I'm not surprised. Few girls would

testify against a man who turned up outside their houses in the dead of night, threatening to murder their families as they slept, quietly reminding them of Lucy Lowe and what happened to her. He only needed to say her name and he'd strike fear into the heart of every girl in the town. I suspect he's still abusing girls in the most horrific way.

I'm not sure what became of Natalie, as we were never really proper mates, but he has probably picked up another vulnerable teenager and persuaded her to help him recruit younger girls as part of his utterly depraved little game. Who knows if he'll ever get caught?

As for Kev, he died suddenly last year. A friend of a friend saw that Nadia had posted news of his demise on Facebook. Beneath his photograph were scores of tributes from friends of the family, saying what a good man he had been, and how he'd be reunited with the love of his life, Liz, who'd died a few years earlier, after years of battling her condition.

The thing that made me most incredulous was seeing someone bleating on about what a great Muslim he was. I almost laughed. I don't claim to be an expert on Islam, but I do know it's supposed to be a peaceful religion and it certainly does not condone, never mind advocate, selling vulnerable young girls for sex for your own financial gain.

So Kev went to his grave without any remorse for what he did to me, or to God knows how many other girls. I'd hazard a guess that he was still trafficking girls to the day he died. I still see some of the men he took me to on the street. The Chinese man with the posh house often shuffles past me, eyes to the ground, as he walks through town with his wife.

I've never seen Lisa around, so I'm not sure if she still lives in the area, or if she and Kev were still together when he died. I do think of her sometimes, and I wonder if she has any remorse for the part she played. Sure, she wasn't there when Kev drove me around and offered me up to the highest bidder, but her comfortable lifestyle depended on men wanting to buy my body and she never did anything to stop it. Saif will be a teenager now and I do wonder what he's turned out like. Hopefully he's very different from his half-brothers.

Speaking of the rest of the family, I'm not sure what's become of Imran or Farooq, but I can't imagine their view of women has changed much. I suppose I feel a little bit sorry for the girls – when I saw Nadia's post, I did wonder if she'd ever had any inkling of how her dad really made his money.

And what of the girls? Carly and I sort of drifted apart after I moved to Oxford with Sanjeev. We didn't fall out or anything, we just gradually stopped speaking as much as we once had. I hate to say it, but I started to realise we didn't actually have that much in common. We were just bound together for so long by a situation that neither of us had chosen. Eventually, she moved abroad and, although we speak occasionally, we're nowhere near as close as we once were. I suppose when I think of her now, I think of the most painful time in my life and it's hard to get past that, as much as it's not her fault.

I heard from a friend that Lily Brown is a recovering drug addict, battling to regain custody of the children she lost to her addiction. Needless to say, she never really got £17,000. Maria, the girl Kev used to replace me, is HIV positive.

Thankfully, my relationship with my family hasn't been ripped apart by what happened to me. I know that many other girls haven't been so fortunate. For a long time, I believe Mum blamed herself for not noticing, and the dynamic of our relationship was a bit strange. I also resented her a little for not picking up on the signs, even though I'd gone out of my way to hide what was happening. But now, we've started to come to terms with what happened. We don't talk about it all that much, but Mum is there for me in lots of other ways. She's the first person I call if I need someone to help with Charlotte and I know she's just round the corner if I have to call on her for any reason.

Liam has struggled to accept what has happened to me, as I imagine any brother would, but I'm more open with my sisters and we're all still close.

There are times when I still struggle to understand what I've been through. Even now, when I think of Beaver, I find it hard to accept he groomed me, abused me and tried to sell me. I know what he did was wrong, but it's a struggle. Psychiatrists might suggest I suffer from a form of Stockholm syndrome, where a hostage feels sympathy towards their captors.

It's even taken me a long time to accept that I wasn't at fault for the worst rapes, or that they were rapes at all. So many people told me I was a slag and a dirty bitch and a prostitute that I believed them.

After a lot of counselling and soul-searching I have come to realise I wasn't any of those things. My counsellors helped me see that I was lured into a world I was too naive to understand, and was taken advantage of in the most merciless way. Now I know I wasn't a child prostitute. There's no such thing; only children who have been horrifically sexually abused and a price put on their heads.

Of course, it's undeniable that the majority of men who abused me were Asian, or born in the UK to Asian parents. I've been courted by lots of racist people, who want to use what happened to me as an excuse to hate an entire continent of people, but I refuse to be a pawn for the far right. There are so many complex cultural issues which could have contributed to what happened to me, but all I know is that when a teenage girl is being pinned to a bed by a whole gang of men, each taking it in turns to violently rape her, the colour of their skin is the last thing on her mind. When I tried to explain this to an activist from the English Defence League, he replied that he hoped my abusers raped my daughter, too. While we have to do our best to understand the reasons for the abuse that I suffered, hating people because of where they come from won't help. It only makes us more bitter and more full of hate and how can we ever work together to find the solution then?

People also ask if I want to see my abusers face justice for what they did to me; if I'll ever go back to the police and ask them to reopen my case. The answer is, I'm not sure. A trial would take up so much of my time and energy, and with a young family it's hard to imagine going back to that dark place. I'd have to relive every detail of those awful years that almost cost me my life, taking to the witness stand and having big-shot defence barristers call me a liar, as Andy or Mr Khan or Beaver, or any one of the scores of men I was sold to, smirked in the dock. Part of me feels like they've already stolen so much of my life that I can't bear it. I don't want my children to see my tear-stained face when I come home from court every day, shaking with horror as the images of those years flash through my mind once more. I know better than most how precious childhood is, and how children should never have to feel that fear and confusion. Could they cope with my nightmares and my flashbacks? Could I?

But I'll never say never, because there might come a day when I change my mind. Right now, all I can do is let these evil men sweat as they wake up every day and wait for that knock at the door. I hope they feel just as scared as I did when they took without asking what should have been the most carefree days of my life.

When I walk past them in the street, I still feel my stomach flutter and my heart pound, but I hold my head high and look them straight in the eye. Most are like the rich Chinese man, in that they look at the ground and pretend I'm not there. They know as well as I do that one phone call to the police could cause their whole life to implode. Most have wives, children and jobs, businesses even, and they'd never recover from the shame their behaviour would bring on their families, if the world were to know.

Back then they thought they were untouchable. They thought no one listened to girls like me. They thought the whole world shared their opinion, that we were worthless little slags, but the tide is turning now. All over the country, the men who did these unthinkable things are seeing their sordid deeds catch up with them, be it in Telford or Rochdale or Rotherham or Oxford. It would only take one call to get the ball rolling again, and I have the power to make it.

Only time will tell if I do pick up the phone. They'll just have to wait to see if I do, and I hope the many sleepless nights they will have along the way will cause them to reflect on what they did. I hope they feel ashamed of what they put me through and I hope the guilt eats them up inside. Because if it doesn't they don't have a shred of humanity in their body.

But no matter how they feel now, they haven't broken me like they thought they might. I'm still here. I have children, a loving partner, and a rewarding career fighting this evil. I'll spend the rest of my life trying to stop this from happening to other children because I want the world to be a better and safer place for my own.

It's been a long journey, but I'm not just a victim, now. I'm also a survivor. And, unlike my innocence, that is something they can never, ever take away from me.

Acknowledgements

I'd like to thank everyone who helped make this book a reality: Jack Falber of Medavia; Clare Hulton, my literary agent, and Kerri Sharp, my editor at Simon & Schuster UK.

I'd also like to thank my family for their continued love and support. I'm also grateful to everyone at Axis Counselling in Telford and the officers who investigated my case.